Able Children

Able Children identifying them in the classroom

Cliff Denton and Keith Postlethwaite

NFER-NELSON

Published by the NFER-NELSON Publishing Company Ltd.,
Darville House, 2 Oxford Road East,
Windsor, Berkshire SL4 1DF
and
242 Cherry Street, Philadelphia, PA 19106 – 1906.
Tel: (215) 238 0939. Telex: 244489.

Library of Congress Cataloging in Publication Data
    Denton, Cliff
        Able Children, Identifying them in the Classroom
        1. Gifted Children – Education – Great Britain.
        2. Gifted Children – identification.
    I. Postlethwaite, Keith.   II. Title.
    LC3997. G7D46   1985   371. 95'2'0941   85-5080
    ISBN 0-7005-0617-9

First Published 1985
© Denton and Postlethwaite 1985
ISBN 0-7005-0617 9
Code 8175 02 1

Photoset by David John (Services) Ltd., Maidenhead

Printed in Great Britain by A. Wheaton & Co. Ltd, Exeter

Contents

Preface

In recent years there has been a sharpening of interest in the education of 'gifted' pupils. One stimulus for this interest is the belief that the education of the 'gifted' to a high level is essential if the complex needs of the society in which we live are to be met, another is the view that these pupils themselves have particular educational needs which society has a duty to meet. In Britain the HMI Reports of 1977 and 1979 revealed that there was a considerable amount of misunderstanding among teachers as to what was meant by the term 'gifted', how the gifted were to be identified in the classroom and what was the appropriate means of educational provision.

This renewed awareness of the problems, albeit in a climate of confusion concerning the meaning of terms such as 'gifted', has been accompanied by the desire of teachers to see the development of effective strategies for the education of children with high ability. The idea that special educational provision for the most able can exist only at the expense of the rest of the pupil population has given way to the view that pupils with high ability exhibit one form of special need which should be met in an appropriate way, as should different categories of special need exhibited by others. This view, consistent with the approach of the recent Warnock Report on Special Educational Needs (1978), has without doubt reinforced a general feeling that 'gifted education' is respectable.

The unfortunate thing is that special education of any kind has to compete for funding with all the other aspects of education. This has meant that initiatives for the more able have necessarily been centred on activities which seem to be most cost effective in terms of educational outcomes. Thus groups of teachers around the country have put their efforts into producing enrichment materials that can be used alongside the normal schoolwork of the children, and into other initiatives such as Summer Schools or Saturday Clubs which for a selection of children enhance existing educational experience. It is instructive to note that many of these initiatives relating to provision for the able child have relied upon teacher-based strategies of identification.

Another consequence of the competition for funds, however, has been that until recently little research work designed to study background issues such as the *effectiveness* of identification and provision strategies has been initiated in Britain. Matters of opinion, rather than hard evidence, are all that has been available. Where they have been based on research at all, these opinions have been based on work that was done some time ago in contexts other than those which exist at present. (In particular, much of our thinking has been influenced by research into general abilities, such as are measured by an IQ test, rather than specific abilities.)

It seemed to us that the time was right to re-examine some of these issues. The Oxford Educational Research Group (OERG) brings together teachers, educational administrators and educational researchers and, supported by the expertise of other specialists at the University, attempts to isolate and tackle questions of practical importance to teachers. Under the auspices of the OERG a small grant was obtained from the Hulme Surplus Fund of Brasenose College so that the background work which would lead to a formal proposal to the Department of Education and Science could be done. A proposal to study the effectiveness of teacher-based identification of pupils with high subject-specific ability was accepted by the DES, who funded a two-year project which began in September 1980 staffed by two research officers and one part-time seconded teacher.

The project focused on 13–14-year-old pupils in four subject areas: mathematics, physics, English and French. We were thus able to make a close study of one year-group of pupils in a representative sample of some important areas of the secondary curriculum. The results are of course directly related to these areas, but it is important to note that there will be much of interest in the research results for teachers of other subjects and of other age groups of pupils.

The final report to the DES was completed in December 1982. It contained large amounts of statistical evidence to support the conclusions that were reached. If this large amount of data were to be reproduced here it would make this book unnecessarily tedious for the general reader who wishes to be informed of the key conclusions which were drawn rather than be led through all of the arguments that led to the conclusions; we have, therefore, been selective in presenting the statistical evidence, but have retained enough to give an appropriate degree of authority to the discussions and conclusions.

We have adopted this more general approach to the text in order to attract a wider readership than a detailed research report might do, because we believe that the key issues have a strong bearing on the everyday practice of a large number of classroom teachers. It is our hope that our work can be of practical support to these teachers who have a central role to play in all aspects of 'gifted education'.

No worthwhile work of this kind would be possible without the cooperation and support of many people. First our thanks must go to the many members of staff in the schools that were at the centre of the work, and to the many colleagues at Oxford and elsewhere who are working on related studies and who gave us sound advice on many key issues. We would like to acknowledge the goodwill of the officers of the Oxfordshire LEA who supported the research in the local schools and who also enabled a number of seconded teachers to work on the project. We also thank these teachers for their valuable work. One in particular should be mentioned by name, Chris Davies whose part-time secondment afforded the necessary expertise in English and French and who carried out much of the fieldwork for these two subjects. A number of colleagues helped with technical aspects of the work and in particular we would like to thank Dr Argyle, Dr Jaspers, Dr Harris and Mr Backhouse. We should also acknowledge the support of the Oxford Examination Board and the Oxford and Cambridge Board for cooperation in the confidential release of examination results, the Computing Division of the Rutherford Laboratory for access to their optical marking system and the administrative and secretarial staff at the University of Oxford Department of Educational Studies for high levels of professionalism in their work for us. We are particularly indebted to the Director of the Department, Dr. Harry Judge, for his unceasing support and confidence, and to Divisional Inspector Tom Marjoram, the chairman of the steering group, who kept us well on course throughout the period of research in the pleasantest of possible styles. Finally we wish to thank the other members of our steering group, all busy people who are experts in their own field, yet who gave of their expertise and time quite freely to see the research through to a satisfactory conclusion: Mr. W.M. Caldow of the DES Administrative Branch, Mr. B.E. Day, the Deputy Chief Education Officer in Oxfordshire, Dr. E.M. Hitchfield, lecturer in Educational Psychology at the Oxford Department of Educational Studies, Dr. D.E.F. Fender, lecturer in Inorganic Chemistry at the University of Oxford, Mr. D.E.R. George, the Dean of Sciences at Nene College, Mr. J.M. Deans, Special Needs Adviser in Oxfordshire and Miss A. Wood, Deputy Headteacher at Milham Ford School, Oxford. To all these people we owe a good deal for their positive contributions to our work and because of the inspiration that has come to us through working with them.

Chapter 1

The Oxford Research Programme

Background to the research questions

The Oxford research programme was concerned with teacher-based identification of pupils with high ability in specific academic subjects. It was focussed on the 'top ten per cent' of 13–14 year old pupils and on the subject areas of mathematics, physics, English and French.

In the Preface reference was made to some of the stimuli which brought life to this research. Amongst these were the HMI reports of 1977 and 1979 which expressed a clear concern about ways of identifying and providing for pupils with high ability in secondary schools. As well as indicating the important issues that should be part of our research programme, these reports provided the background to decisions such as the size of the target population and the subject-specific nature of the enquiry.

Although the 1979 HMI survey was not exclusively concerned with more able pupils, it was interesting to see that it reflected, on a national scale, evidence of the same concerns about able children that were expressed to us by teachers in Oxfordshire who were interviewed as one of the preliminary steps in our research. For example, HMI, regarding the need for greater stimulus for the more able in mathematics, stated that:

> Appropriate provision for these abler pupils (whether future students of A-level mathematics or not) could involve an extension of the ordinary syllabus, but the greater need relates to

outlook, pace and variety of application. The pupils require a challenge to work in different ways; there should be more opportunity for extended investigations of topics which catch the imagination, and much more encouragement to undertake supplementary reading.

Again, writing of science, HMI commented:

In about one third of all schools it was apparent that insufficient demands were made of able pupils. For example, those who finished practical work long before the rest of the class were frequently left with nothing to do when perhaps additional experimental work of a problem solving kind could have challenged them and tested their abilities to the full.

There was, therefore, no doubt that questions relating to more able pupils could be seen as examples of contemporary concern at national as well as local level. Importantly, there was a clear indication that specific subjects provided the most appropriate context for studying these questions. This indication came from a number of directions; teachers themselves who were interviewed in the early stages of our own work considered that research concerned with children with high ability should be related to the course of study on which the children were engaged. This was amplified on a national scale by the HMI reports themselves which to a large extent took on a subject-specific focus. Furthermore, there was considerable support for this subject-specific focus from a great deal of psychological literature which added theoretical stability to the practical perspective.

The 1979 HMI survey also provided support for the teachers' view that a relatively large group of pupils should be considered as more able. It is not easy to be clear from the report *exactly* the proportion of pupils to which HMI were referring when they wrote of the problems of the more able, but there is a strong implication that it was a fairly large group of perhaps 15 per cent of the population in a school. What is quite clear is that HMI were not commenting on just the top 2 per cent (for there is a separate Appendix to the report that deals with these pupils). Further independent support for the study of a fairly large group of pupils is also provided by other workers in the field such as Renzulli and colleagues (1981) in their 'Revolving Door Model' of identification.

From our visits to the schools that were to take part in our own research it became clear that one particular question in the general area of concern about more able pupils in a given subject was repeatedly being brought to our attention. This was the question of how such pupils are to be *identified* for any additional or alternative activities which might be arranged in an attempt to make their educational curriculum more appropriate to their special needs. Again, there was broad support for the idea that identification did indeed pose a problem. In their report specifically about gifted children, HMI (1977) recommended that a systematic screening procedure should be evident in every school but reported that this did not generally exist. They commented that:

> There is no overall policy for identification. Identification is a hit and miss affair, the initiative coming mainly from individual teachers.

HMI's support for the idea that identification should be carried out on a subject-specific basis can be seen in the fact that the second section of the report is divided into chapters which deal separately with different subjects. Most of these chapters make direct reference to how pupils, more able in that subject, could be recognized. The rich diversity of characteristics listed in this part of the report gives great weight to the idea that ability in one subject may not necessarily go hand in hand with ability in another.

Thus, discussions with teachers at a local level coupled with the HMI reports led to the view that important work could be done relating to the identification of more able pupils, that this should be done in a subject-specific context and that the target group for such a study should be fairly large.

It is interesting to draw attention at this point to the fact that there is evidence of a very considerable shift in the attitudes of teachers towards gifted children over the last decade. This change to a situation in which teachers are more favourably disposed towards the idea of considering the more able as a group which does have special needs in education is in itself important, as it implies that teachers will seize on new information in the under-researched areas of how effectively to identify and provide for these children, and draw it into their future practice. The position in the early 1970s was recently described in an article by Ogilvie (1980):

The position in schools in 1970 with regard to the concept of 'giftedness' almost defied description. Some teachers felt very strongly that the whole idea smacked of elitism, and hence were reluctant even to discuss it; others were equally certain that the only real difficulty lay in problems of reliability of intelligence tests.

Our discussions suggested that this was no longer an accurate indication of the way teachers thought about gifted children. They were no longer strait-jacketed by the concept of intelligence testing. They were also much more favourably disposed towards the general question of making provision for the gifted. Positive attitudes, similar to those which we met, were also reported by Tilsley (1979).

The reasons for the change in general attitude over ten years are no doubt complex and we will not attempt to trace them in detail here. One component may be that a technique of making provision for the gifted, now commonly recommended, is that of supplying the teacher with challenging materials which might extend the work of such children in ordinary classes. The use of these 'enrichment materials' raises fewer problems of elitism in the minds of teachers than did earlier suggestions for provision, which tended to lay emphasis on techniques such as acceleration of 'express streams' and were therefore either limited in application to a smaller range of pupils or had significant resource implications. Tilsley's study offers some support for the idea that teachers' attitudes are significantly influenced by the resource issue. Another component, however, seems to be that teachers are becoming increasingly interested in the importance of trying to meet an individual pupil's particular educational needs, wherever that pupil lies on the spectrum of abilities. Work with the gifted is therefore often viewed as one aspect of a much wider activity aimed at meeting the whole range of special needs. It has therefore become linked in the mind, and sometimes in the school (though not according to the letter of the law), with work aimed at the very different groups of children who are the subjects of the 1981 Education Act. This, we suggest, is a very proper link which may well provide an environment in which the present positive attitudes towards the gifted will be encouraged to grow.

Reasons for the increased willingness to think in terms other than general intelligence are also difficult to trace. Perhaps the subject-based projects for gifted children which have sprung up around the country have had some impact on the attitudes of a wider group of teachers than the group actively involved. Perhaps the changing general attitudes have encouraged teachers to think about how they could help to provide for more able pupils, and this has driven them towards a subject-specific model. On the other hand it may be the preparedness of teachers to accept a subject-specific model that has encouraged them to move towards a more positive general attitude. Whatever the relationship between cause and effect is, however, there is no doubt that many teachers are anxious for guidance in relation to the education of their pupils of highest ability, so that effective strategies can be implemented. Undoubtedly one of their major concerns is centred on the nature of effective identification strategies.

Among those possible, one identification strategy that relies at least in part on teacher judgement has been commonly proposed by those working with enrichment programmes for the gifted. Unfortunately, because of the size of the task none of these projects has been able to include a research element in their work so that although strong arguments can be constructed in support of teacher involvement, little has been available as evidence for or against the hypothesis that teachers are effective agents in the identification process. Teacher-based identification of the more able has much to commend it if it can be shown to be effective. It is an identification strategy which can be constantly amended by an up to date knowledge of the subject-specific abilities of children as they develop. However, both individual teachers and organizers of major initiatives for the gifted have voiced uncertainties, so that a clear desire has been expressed for an appropriate research initiative in this direction.

At this point it is appropriate to describe the research carried out at Oxford between 1980 and 1982 in an attempt to provide answers to some of these questions. On the basis of the wide set of data that was gathered and the extensive analysis that was carried out, this research has put us in a position to give guidance on many of the important issues associated with effective identification strategies in the secondary school. In particular, we can discuss the issues of test-based and teacher-based identification strategies, including how accurate each might be; the way in which aptitudes related to a particular subject can be put together to form a 'checklist' which can be used to assist a teacher in the identification process and the limitations of such an approach; and also the important relationship between effective identification and effective provision. As explained in the Preface to this book, our focus will not be so much on the analysis of our data and justification of our methods, but on a discussion of the findings of our work, relating them to the practical concerns of a teacher faced with the task of identifying pupils with high ability in a subject. We aim to provide a digestible amount of evidence in support of our findings – enough to illustrate our points, but not enough to overburden the reader with detail; however, before we begin this task it is necessary to describe the general design of the research programme so that the reader can relate the findings to the background work. The rest of the present chapter, therefore, will be devoted to this description.

The Oxford research programme

The first phase of the study was concerned with the levels of agreement between test-based measures of potential in a subject and teacher judgement of which pupils had high potential in that subject. This took on the nature of a large statistical exercise.

Four subjects were chosen, important in their own right, but also representing major areas of the secondary curriculum. These were English, mathematics, physics (for the sciences) and French (for the languages). We suggest that the conclusions might be extended with caution to similar subjects but a large-scale generalization to all subjects, especially to those outside the academic areas of the curriculum, would not be wise.

The specific questions that we set out to tackle in the first phase were:

1. To what extent do tests and teachers agree when judgements of subject-specific potential are made?

2. In so far as judgements of accuracy are possible, is there cause for concern regarding the accuracy of teachers' nominations for high ability groups?

3. Are the characteristics of the pupils selected by teachers appropriate, or is it possible to detect unfavourable influences on teachers' identification strategies?

4. If teachers use checklists of subject-specific aptitudes to assist them, does this make their identification any more effective?

There were a number of decisions to be made in relation to these questions.

a. What types of schools should be studied and compared?

b. What age group of pupils should be studied?

c. What proportion of children should be taken as 'more able' for the purposes of the study?

d. What should be taken as the criterion used for labelling pupils as 'more able' in each subject; and how should the effectiveness of teachers in identifying such pupils be assessed?

e. How should a valid checklist be compiled?

f. How should the effectiveness of checklists as guides to teachers be assessed?

In this chapter we will discuss our approach to all of these issues except the development of the checklists, which is reserved for the next chapter.

The sample of schools

The selection of schools for this study was made through negotiation with head teachers and heads of department. A selection of secondary schools were chosen, essentially at random, and meetings were arranged with headteachers to seek their involvement. Of 12 schools that were approached 11 opted into the research programme. In this way we managed to gain the cooperation of an approximately proportional stratified sample of schools in Oxfordshire. The total number of schools was large enough to include a number of different types, but not so large as to be unmanageable with regard to staffing available for the study. Tables 1.1 to 1.4 give the number of schools of each type in the county of Oxfordshire and in the sample.

Tables 1.1–1.4:   Numbers of schools of each kind in the county and in the sample

Table 1.1

		13–18 AGE GROUP		11–18 AGE GROUP	
		County	Sample	County	Sample
1000 or fewer pupils*	Boys	1	1	1	0
	Girls	1	1	0	0
	Mixed	5	1	15	2
1001–1500 pupils	Boys	0	0	0	0
	Girls	0	0	1	0
	Mixed	1	0	15	5
1500 plus pupils	Boys	0	0	0	0
	Girls	0	0	0	0
	Mixed	0	0	2	1

* One sample school is mixed, 11–16 with 1000 or fewer pupils

Table 1.2			**Table 1.3**			**Table 1.4**		
	County	Sample		County	Sample		County	Sample
Mixed*	38	9	13–18	8	3	1000*	23	5
Single sex	4	2	11–18 *	34	8	1000+	19	6

* One sample school is 11–16

It turned out that the school with more than 1500 pupils was made up of three lower school (11–15 years) halls and an upper school (16–18 years). In many ways these halls functioned as separate schools, and independent judgements were made about more able pupils in each hall. We took account of this in our analysis when appropriate, so that tables will sometimes show figures for 13 schools rather than 11.

The schools were coded numerically (00 to 13, schools 10, 11, and 12 being the three units of school 13).

In order to assess the effectiveness of checklists in their preliminary form, the schools were divided into two groups which we will call 'Experimental' and 'Control'. Early in the school year all schools were asked to identify more able pupils without any guidance from checklists. A term later, all schools were asked to make a second identification. This time the experimental schools used subject-specific checklists, while the control schools worked without such guidance.

Table 1.5 gives a complete classification of the schools appropriate to our work.

Table 1.5: School involvement in the first phase

	Category	Experimental	Control
11+	Large	13	
	Medium	01, 04	00, 06, 07
	Small	03,	08
13+		02	05, 09

Note: School 02 is single sex (boys), School 05 is single sex (girls).

The sample of pupils

TARGET AGE GROUP

Rather than make a superficial study of children over a wide age range, we selected one group – arguably a particularly important group – and subjected these to a more detailed study. The firm conclusions that emerge from a detailed study of one age group might then reasonably be generalized to other age groups in which the teaching/learning environment is reasonably similar.

For this study, then, we selected and focused on third form pupils (13–14 year olds). There were a number of reasons for this choice. It is an age group of children in which we could confidently assume that at least the top ten per cent would have reached the Piagetian Stage of Formal Operational Thought. Their ability to work with mathematical and scientific abstractions and generalizations would enable us to refer to broader aspects of subject-specific ability (e.g. in our work on checklists) than might be possible with younger children. The third year is a time when the levels of challenge that could be met by the top ten per cent of children (our target group) are, in a number of subjects, drawing noticeably apart from the levels suitable for other pupils. At this age, then, a fairly large group of able children should be recognizable and be ready for a higher level of subject-specific challenge.

A second reason why the third year was a good choice was a practical one. It is common practice for pupils to make their final selections of optional subjects during their third form. This is, therefore, a critical year for the assessment of pupils' abilities by subject teachers, so that proper guidance can be given. All schools feel the need for accurate assessment strongly, particularly in the upper schools where 13–14 year olds are embarking on their first year at the school after moving up from middle schools. Thus in asking teachers to identify more able pupils in the third year we were asking them only to engage in an extension of a process which is already accepted as a sensible and necessary part of the normal routine of the school.

There were further pragmatic reasons why the choice of year group was no later than the third form in our research. In view of the final two years of preparation for public examinations it would not have been acceptable to those who cooperated with us to impose a large research effort on pupils in their fourth or fifth years.

As we have suggested, a case could be argued for a study of any year group in the secondary school, but we feel that the reasons given above make the choice of the third year most appropriate.

THE SIZE OF THE 'MORE ABLE' GROUP

The next consideration was the size of the target group. HMI expressed concern, confirmed by the teachers who took part in our preliminary discussions, that a group much wider than the traditional 'gifted' group of about two per cent were being underchallenged in school. Thus it was desirable that our research into identification should also take in a wider group. The final choice was inevitably arbitrary to some extent, but the top ten per cent seems an appropriate group. This group of course includes the top five per cent and other smaller subgroups, and the research was structured so that relevant work could be done on these narrower target groups. In the schools in which we worked, the top ten per cent was of the order of 10–20 pupils, who would, therefore, comprise the top half of the top teaching set in a year group of a school that divided its pupils into ability groups at third form level. Because the needs of particular children will clearly depend on the context in which they are educated, we decided to define the group relative to their peers in their own school. It would have been a much more difficult and less meaningful exercise if the teachers had been asked to nominate the top percentiles on national norms. Although the 'top ten per cent' in one school may differ in absolute ability from the 'top ten per cent' in another, it is likely that both groups, being well above average in their own environment, may have need of some special provision.

We will go on to list the full test battery that was administered to the pupils but at this point it is appropriate to give some background statistics regarding the pupil sample. The means and standard deviations for the whole sample of pupils on the set of Differential Aptitude (DAT) Tests that were administered to the pupils are given in Table 1.6 and the distribution of social class is given in Table 1.7. Among the schools was one (07) in which there was a bias of social class towards the manual end of the social class spectrum (classes IV and V). The distribution of social class in School 07 was as follows.

Class	I	II	III	IV	V
Number	2	27	136	53	15

This distribution is heavily weighted away from the high social classes (classes I and II). It is significantly different from the rest of the sample ($\chi^2 = 47.27$, df = 4, p<.001) and a considerable number of pupils come from the low social classes.

The DAT scores of the overall sample were close to the DAT national norms, so that we might expect to have a proportion of

Table 1.6:   Means and standard deviations of whole sample on DAT scores

DIFFERENTIAL APTITUDE SCORES (First phase of study)

	Sample			National Norms		
	mean	sd	n	mean	sd	n
VR	22.1	8.89	2151	22.5	10.0	2394
NA	13.4	6.44	2157	12.9	6.6	2396
VN	35.5	13.82	2148	35.4	15.2	2394
AR	30.9	9.82	2147	29.7	11.0	2402
CSA	42.5	11.97	2149	38.2	11.9	2339
MR	41.0	9.95	2158	39.5	9.8	2339
SR	29.3	10.58	2167	26.4	10.2	2379
SP	56.1	15.87	2162	55.5	16.2	2377
LU	26.5	9.28	2165	25.9	9.6	2375

VR: Verbal Reasoning
NA: Numerical Ability
VN = VR+NA: A General Ability
    Measure
AR: Abstract Reasoning

MR: Mechanical Reasoning
SR: Space Relations
SP: Spelling
LU: Language Usage
CSA: Clerical Speed and Accuracy

Table 1.7:   Frequency distribution in the sample of registrar general classification

Class	I	II	III	IV	V
Number	118	440	1108	270	73
Percentage of total	6	22	55	13	4

children of high ability according to *national* norms within our sample. Table 1.7 is weighted a little towards the professional end of the scale so that our results, as a whole, may not be generalizable to all schools (such as some inner city schools in deprived areas), though the inclusion of one school, where the weighting was to the other end of the scale, could provide some clues about schools of that type.

Background criterion

We will now discuss the issue of what should be used as a background criterion against which to assess the effectiveness of teachers nominating high ability groups. Clearly some alternative means of assessing the abilities of children had to be developed, otherwise it would not have been possible to make judgements about the teachers' success in nominating these groups. The decision as to what this background criterion might be, however, was by no means easy to make.

There were a number of points to consider. The first centred on a decision about what we actually *mean* by 'high ability' in a subject. The second was that it had to be practicable to construct a background criterion measure in relation to this definition of high ability. The third was that teacher-based identification at third form level should be a meaningful activity in relation to this definition. Importantly, in this context, both background criterion and teacher assessment should be concerned with the same definition of high ability. Fourth, it was necessary to apply this background criterion in a meaningful way to a group as wide as the top ten per cent in a subject and also to the narrow band of pupils at the top end of this group; that is, it was necessary to distinguish pupils of different abilities within the top ten per cent groups without making the criterion inappropriate at the ten per cent borderline.

We decided that the background criterion should be associated with prediction for future performance, particularly as we considered that children at third form level have the major stepping stones to realizing their potential ahead of them. Quite clearly, however, a background criterion by which pupils were assessed for such high-level goals as, say, membership of the Royal Society would not have been meaningful across the ten per cent group, and neither would teachers have found this a meaningful criterion when judging pupils at third form level. Indeed it could be argued that there is such a large degree of uncertainty associated with the identification of suitable pupils for long-term goals of this kind that it would be impracticable for a teacher to attempt to nominate, out of a small group of pupils who had the ability to attain such long-term goals, those who would actually reach them. Because of the limited number of positions which could be considered to represent the highest attainment in the pursuit of excellence available in our society, 'chance' might arguably have a part to play in the fulfilment of potential for these positions. On the other hand children who had a potential for a significant contribution to knowledge in the subjects of our study would come within the top ten per cent group and our background criterion should place them at the top of this group, even though it might not be possible to forecast which of these pupils would go on to choose or have the opportunity to make these contributions in the long term.

A consideration of the alternatives available drew us to consider not only a measure of potential which was associated more with the short-term goals of the pupils' course of study, but also one with predictive value for more distant goals. It was clear that *teachers* of thirteen-year-olds had the goal of O-level, two years ahead, in mind when they made assessments of ability, so providing that we could interpret this goal in a meaningful way this could reasonably be taken as the basis of a background criterion. As we shall see, it was possible to derive subject-specific predictors for O-level *marks* for each of the pupils in each of the four subjects that were studied (and to do so with a known average error of estimation).

Now one could argue that pupils who achieved marks which placed them near the pass/fail boundary at O-level could have reached this standard with only a basic understanding of the subject. However, it is not likely that a pupil will achieve the highest marks within the highest grade unless he/she has exercised the full range of aptitudes for the subject in question to a high level relative to other pupils of a similar age. By considering the potential of a pupil in relation to an O-level *mark* rather than a grade, therefore, we hoped that the background criterion would meet the fourth point which we mentioned above, namely that it could meaningfully be applied to the whole of the ten per cent group, retaining the necessary precision to distinguish pupils with the highest potential in the group.

Of course, it must be admitted that the O-level criterion would not have been as satisfactory had our interest been in just the pupils of the highest potential, say the top 0.1 per cent. Arguably it would be extremely difficult (and perhaps impossible) to design such a criterion for use with thirteen-year-olds.

By designing test-based measures of O-level potential, using these to produce test-based nominations for the top ten per cent target group and comparing these nominations with other nominations produced by teachers, our research was able to shed light directly on teachers' ability to identify pupils with high potential for O-level performance.

There is some support for the view that high ability at O-level can be used as an indicator of high ability in a broader sense. This can be found in work which attempts to measure the predictive validity of O-level itself. There is evidence to suggest that O-level performance in a subject is highly correlated with later performance on more demanding criteria in the same subject. Murphy (1981), for example, has found the following high correlations between O-level and A-level marks:

Subject	No. pupils	Pearson correlation[1]
English	3462	0.63
French	1688	0.90
Physics	3407	0.81
Mathematics	3110	0.81

If one is prepared to accept this kind of evidence for the predictive validity of O-level scores, our study can be taken as providing some information on the effectiveness of teachers in identifying pupils who have high ability in this broader sense. In interpreting our results in this way it would be important to take account of the error of the O-level result in predicting for whatever later measure of attainment we might have in mind. No attempt has been made to do so in this book (though our own treatment of the error associated with our test-based assessment of O-level performance might provide a means by which the job could be done). We would, however, argue that this error in the predictive validity of O-level will not be so large as to invalidate the main thrust of our conclusions.

Any study can only provide *evidence* rather than *proof*, and the task of the researcher is to maximize the strength of the evidence by making the research instruments as sharp as possible, and then, based on evidence from a number of complementary directions, assess the general impact of this evidence and go on to reason out sound recommendations within the limits of the evidence. Because of the insights gained from one component of the work, one set of

---

[1] Corrected for limited range of O-level marks of those entered for A-level

recommendations might suggest that a complementary piece of research be carried out in a certain area to clarify an issue and enable more detailed conclusions to be drawn.

Finally we should point out why we used test-based measures of potential at third form level as a background criterion rather than using the actual O-level scores which pupils achieved two years later. This was partly because we felt it was preferable to derive predicted scores for a whole year-group rather than study the final results of only a limited number of pupils who were entered for the examination. Furthermore, we conjectured that many pupils in this small sample might not have realized their true potential because of the many factors which come into play between the third and fifth forms at school, rendering many of their actual O-level scores less precise measures of potential than those we derived at third form level. To add to the precision of our conclusions we derived methods of accounting for test error of our predicted scores. This would not have been possible with actual results.

Having argued why O-level potential was taken as our background criterion for the first phase, it remains to explain how prediction for O-level success was achieved. This will be done in the next chapter.

Survey of the main activities for the first phase of the research

At this point it will be useful to give an outline of the research design for the first phase, which was carried out over one school year.

Our questions related to two sorts of teacher-based identification of top ability groups, the first unaided and the second after the use of checklists. The checklist-aided identification during this phase can be considered as a preliminary to the more detailed work that followed. We state this with hindsight, because the second phase of the work attempted to gain insights into questions shown up by the first phase. A particularly important aspect of the first phase was that we asked teachers to use checklists in the way that they would normally do if they were following the guidelines set out in the growing amount of literature on the subject. Because of this, the initial insights have practical relevance in their own right.

In the autumn term of 1980 all schools in our sample were asked to identify their groups of pupils of high ability in each subject without any guidance from checklists. These data were used to assess the accuracy of unguided teacher-based identification. In preparation for the work on the value of checklists, schools were then divided at random into experimental and control groups. Base line comparisons between the effectiveness of teachers in the two groups of schools, later to be used as control and experimental schools, were then made.

In the spring term of 1981 all schools were asked to make a second identification. This time the experimental schools used the subject-specific checklists, whereas the control schools, again, worked without any such guidance. Comparisons between the same two groups of schools were then made in respect of the spring round of identification to establish whether the checklists, used in the experimental schools in this round, had contributed to the change in effectiveness of the teachers in those schools. The use of a group of control schools enabled us to separate any effect which was due to the use of checklists from any effect which might have arisen simply through the greater length of time that the teachers had had to get to know their pupils. Though the gap of only a term between the two rounds of identification in one sense is rather small if we are looking at changes in teachers' ability to recognize their able pupils, a moment's thought will reveal that the identifications were made at two key times, the first at the beginning of an important school year and the second at a time when pupils would be asked to commit themselves to their choice of subjects for later study at school. Furthermore, we were comparing two different methods of identification (one without, the other with checklists). Had the gap of time been larger we might have discovered the effect of checklists to be swamped by the knowledge of pupils gained in the normal way. The important thing was that teachers were given sufficient time to work with checklists. It turned out that there was approximately six months between the two rounds.

The next issue was that of how to gain insights into the kinds of pupils identified by teachers. These would be of interest in their own right and, interpreted with caution, might give some ideas about the process which leads teachers to make judgements about whether or not a pupil was in the 'top ten per cent' group. We tackled this in two ways. First, on the basis of the individual background test scales, we made comparisons between pupils who were identified by their teachers and pupils who had similar potential for the subject but who were overlooked by their teachers. (We looked, for example, at the numbers of boys and girls who were identified and at the numbers who were overlooked to see if there was any evidence that the sex of a pupil was associated with selection for the top ability lists by his/her teachers.) The second and more direct method of enquiring into the process which led teachers to their overall judgement involved interviews with them in which we asked them to talk about the characteristics of particular pupils. By suggesting the names of pupils who were correctly identified, overestimated or underestimated by teachers, we gained some insights into the kinds of pupil characteristics which teachers noticed, and were able to form some tentative views about how these characteristics affected teachers as they made their judgements. This phase of work opened up related questions and a new line of research for the second phase, which we will now describe.

The second phase of the research

By this stage we had assembled a large amount of statistical evidence concerning the relationship between teacher selection of able pupils and test scores. Apart from the very open-ended interviews, however, there had been no direct study of either the pupils or their teachers.

Two main questions were unanswered at the end of this work. One was related to checklist usage. In the way in which we had asked teachers to use them, checklists did not appear to be effective instruments. One reason may have been that the detailed clues to ability referred to by the lists could not be picked up in the restrictive environment of the classroom, because the pupils were not provided with the sort of work that would enable them to display such clues. An alternative reason, however, could have been that the way in which the checklists had been used had been inappropriate. We suspected from our discussions with the teachers concerned that the former possibility was very likely, but that the method of checklist usage might also be changed so that clues to ability that did occur might be recorded more effectively.

The other question not resolved at the end of the first phase was concerned with pupil characteristics which were associated with (and may have influenced) teachers' judgements. Our evidence was necessarily limited to information related to our test battery, enhanced to some extent by responses to our interviews with teachers about the sorts of characteristics they noticed in the pupils. However, the interviews were deliberately conducted in a very open-ended way, and something with a more precise structure was called for if any firm conclusions were to be drawn.

One of the main activities of the second phase was restricted to just one subject – mathematics. The work was centred on extensive classroom observations which, we hoped, would provide insights into the question of whether the relevant clues to ability could emerge from the day to day activity. The other major second phase activity involved a much more structured approach to an investigation into the nature of the pupil characteristics to which teachers were sensitive when making their judgements about pupils. This was based on personal construct methodology (Kelly, 1955). From this we hoped to discover the scope of teachers' knowledge of pupils as they attempted to make their identifications.

Thus we moved away from an approach based on statistical analysis and took a closer look at the classroom, so that we could add the necessary evidence which might allow us to make more balanced judgements concerning the problems and possibilities associated with teacher-based identification strategies.

We have described the research phases in some detail so that the reader might be aware of the way the research programme evolved and how our investigations led us towards sets of complementary clues concerning the effectiveness of teacher-based identification of the more able.

Having assembled the evidence, however, we find we can look at it in relation to the major issues in a variety of ways. In a book of this kind it is more useful to discuss these issues under separate headings than it would be to report on the mixture of clues as they emerged from the research. Readers should be able to decide for themselves how each piece of data emerged from the research, and with the reasoning of this chapter in the background we hope readers will gain the same level of confidence in our conclusions that we have ourselves.

Chapter 2

Who Are The Gifted?

One component of the insecurity that teachers feel in their work with gifted children is related to the fact that a certain amount of ambiguity has crept into the term 'gifted' over the last three or four decades. As our understanding of the structure of human abilities has deepened, and our views about the legitimate aims of schooling have broadened, definitions of the gifted have changed. The ambiguities have arisen as a result of this change. While some educationalists have accepted a wider definition others continue to use the term 'gifted' in its traditional sense, leaving those who are not experts in the field but who would wish to recognize and nurture the 'gifted' children that appear in their classrooms confused and insecure.

There is little doubt that a neat definition of giftedness based on the possession of a high score on a measure of general ability (say a score of 140+ on an IQ test), although once accepted, is no longer deemed to be adequate. Instead the view that children may be very able at some worthwhile activities and not so able at others has led to a wider perspective of giftedness. To define giftedness in a wider sense is more complex in terms of background psychological theory, however, and there is still a good deal of work to be done before there is final agreement concerning the background components of human abilities. Nevertheless there is already a good deal of evidence to support a subject-specific element in a definition of giftedness. This has important consequences for those who teach individual subjects within a school curriculum; the implication is that a search for children who have high ability in a particular subject, irrespective of their abilities in others, is at least as valid a search for 'giftedness' as is a search for those who are generally most able.

At this stage it would be helpful to describe the development of alternative definitions of giftedness and indicate how the broader and most widely accepted definitions in current use have emerged. Our thinking must go back to the beginning of the twentieth century, when the understanding of the nature of human abilities was in a rudimentary state, when valid tests of intelligence had not been devised and when matters of opinion, some of which now seem absurd, were the only basis for understanding.

The work of Terman and his associates (1925, 1926, 1930, 1947, 1959), whose long-term, large-scale study of 'gifted people' in America marked the beginning of scientific study of 'giftedness', has had an impact on the field which is still being felt. They defined a gifted child as one who, on the Stanford-Binet Intelligence Scale, achieved a score above a certain cut-off point. They used different cut-offs for different age groups, but most of their 'gifted group' had IQ scores above 140 and lay within the top one per cent of the school population of equivalent age, based on this test scale.

Their work had an enormous impact. They overthrew the idea of 'early ripe – early rot' and challenged the idea of the supposed relationship between genius and madness which had held sway earlier (see for example Lombroso, 1891, *The Man of Genius* and Nisbet, 1895, *The Insanity of Genius*). They dispelled belief in the caricature of the gifted child as a socially inadequate, physically incompetent and emotionally unstable being and in their own study found evidence that such children were:

> appreciably superior to unselected (i.e. IQ less than 140) children in physique, health and social adjustment, markedly superior in moral attitudes . . . and vastly superior in the mastery of school subjects.

It was natural that a massive innovatory study such as Terman's should generate much similar activity, and with a well developed test that could be used to identify children of high IQ, important research into the characteristics of this kind of gifted child flourished. Notable contributions to work in this field were provided by, among others, Hollingworth (1942), Parkyn (1948), Lovell and Shields (1967). There was considerable agreement between these researchers as to the characteristics of this kind of gifted child and in consequence the picture that their work painted of such children has become widely accepted.

As this work continued, however, a certain amount of critical interest was expressed in the fact that there was such great emphasis placed on the single criterion of high IQ. One aspect of this concern rested upon the fact that the cut-off point for a pupil to be included in the gifted group was arbitrarily defined. However, an even more serious concern was expressed by workers who felt that the emphasis on the single dimension of IQ was unhelpfully restrictive. Witty (1951) suggested that we should move away from an IQ based definition of giftedness towards a much broader view. He offered, as an alternative, the suggestion that 'the definition of the gifted be expanded to include any child whose performance in a worthwhile type of human endeavour is consistently or repeatedly remarkable'.

Getzels and Jackson (1958) made a considerable contribution to the argument that undue emphasis should not be put on IQ, writing that 'it not only restricts our perspective of the more general phenomenon, but places on the one concept a greater theoretical and predictive burden than it was intended to carry'.

Important theoretical support for the evolution of these broader concepts of giftedness was to be found in studies which attempted to explore the structure of human ability and to isolate its separate components. Such attempts have a long history. In the light of the work of Torrance (1961) and Getzels and Jackson (1962) the idea grew that 'creativity' was one such component. The evidence for its existence as an ability which can be to some extent distinct from general ability added much to the debate. In the context of our interest in how to identify the 'gifted' it is important to note that the latter researchers indicated not only that many highly creative pupils would be overlooked by IQ tests but also that such pupils tended to be unpopular with teachers – and so might easily be overlooked if identification was to be based on teachers' judgements.

However, important though the concept of creativity is, it is not the only additional component of ability which needs to be considered. Thurstone's (1941) suggestion that the IQ test itself was a composite of many cognitive tests raised the possibility that a more systematic mapping of the cognitive domain might bring to light several quite specific forms of cognitive ability. Guilford (1959, 1967) provides the most extreme example of the outcome of such a mapping. He suggests that the intellect is made up of 120 separate specific abilities, and has produced tests which seem to measure many of them in isolation. His view has been severely criticised by some. Eysenck (1967) suggests that the statistical technique is capable of infinite subdivision, that the model is a poor predictor and that it omits the essentially hierarchical nature of the data. Guilford himself admits that the details of his model 'may or may not stand the test of time' though he does go on to say that the underlying principle of the 'multiplicity of intellectual abilities seems well established' (Guilford, in Barbe and Renzulli, 1975). There is clearly much more work to be done to establish the exact relationship between general ability (measured by IQ) and specific abilities (such as are suggested by the Guilford model). Until this relationship is known, we should consider the relevance of both of the models to any study of children with high ability.

There is no doubt that there is a widespread acceptance of a multi-dimensional model of the intellect, whatever the final details might be, so that an allowance for specific abilities, whatever their relationship to the 'g' factor, must be made in our quest for full understanding of human abilities. An important point is that in schools we nurture pupils in the specific abilities appropriate to individual subjects, so that it is fitting to make use of the specific ability model.

Recent writers have attempted to develop the multi-dimensional philosophy. In an influential report to Congress, the US Commissioner for Education gave the following definition of the gifted (Marland, 1972):

[They have] high demonstrated achievement, and/or potential in any of the following areas, singly or in combination:
  general intellectual ability
  specific academic aptitude
  creative or productive thinking
  leadership ability
  visual and performing arts
  psychomotor ability.

In Britain, a little later, Ogilvie (1973) suggested the following definition of the gifted pupil.

The term 'gifted' is used to indicate any child who is outstanding in either a general or specific ability, in a relatively broad or narrow field of endeavour . . . Where generally recognized tests exist as (say) in the case of 'intelligence', then 'giftedness' would be defined by test scores. Where no recognized tests exist it can be assumed that the subjective opinions of 'experts' in the various fields on the creative qualities of originality and imagination displayed would be the criteria we have in mind.

And more recently still, Kerry (1981) wrote:

We shall call 'bright' any child with IQ in the region of 130 or one who shows an outstanding talent in any one field of schoolwork which sets him or her notably above other pupils in the class or age-group.

Such definitions suggest that the subject-specific focus that we were urged to adopt for our own study, and which we recommend to teachers, was a reasonable one in that pupils with high potential in a specific subject would certainly fall within the 'gifted groups' proposed by these definitions. What the definitions also did, of course, was to warn us that anyone working with able children would usually need to make a decision as to what was the most appropriate part of the 'gifted' definition for their own purposes. A study such as ours, related to a subject-specific notion of giftedness, would have psychological respectability because of recent research but would be only one of the possible focuses of attention. It should not be regarded as an attempt to support or refute the findings of the earlier studies on children with high IQ, nor should it be rashly generalized to all parts of, say, Marland's definition. It is simply an attempt to shed light on one part of the gifted field which has not been extensively researched in the past.

At this point it is interesting to ask whether our decision to adopt a subject-specific focus made any practical difference to the matter of which pupils came under our scrutiny. Were the pupils listed as more able in one subject substantially the same as those listed in another? The following tables shed some light on this issue.

We recall that teachers were asked to nominate the top ten per cent of pupils in each of four subjects and parallel test-based assessments of potential were also made. Table 2.1 shows the percentages of children selected as being in the top ten per cent in terms of O-level potential in one particular subject, who were also selected as being in the top ten per cent in another subject. Thus, for example, 56 per cent of the pupils categorized (on this criterion) as 'more able' in English were also categorized as being 'more able' in French.

Table 2.1: Percentage of pupils nominated for the top ten per cent in one subject who were also nominated for another (Test figures shown; teacher figures in brackets)

Nominated in	Percentage also nominated in		
	French	*Physics*	*Maths*
English	63%(56)	45%(52)	55%(49)
	English	*Physics*	*Maths*
French	63%(61)	40%(46)	56%(56)
	English	*French*	*Maths*
Physics	45%(51)	44%(54)	67%(50)
	English	*French*	*Physics*
Maths	53%(48)	45%(54)	66%(51)

These figures are based on work done in eleven schools with approximately 2300 third form pupils. It is interesting to note that there was indeed a substantial lack of agreement between the lists of pupils recognised as 'more able' in one subject, and the corresponding list for another subject. There was substantial agreement between teachers and tests on this issue.

Table 2.2 completes the picture. To obtain the figures for this table we listed all pupils who appeared on any of the four top ten per cent lists, noting on how many lists each name appeared. We then calculated the percentage of all named pupils who were nominated in only one, in two and only two, in three and only three, or in all four subjects.

As for the preceding table, figures based on both teacher nominations and test-based nominations are shown. There is again considerable agreement between teachers and tests that relatively few children are in the top ability bands on all four subjects compared, in particular, with the numbers able in just one of the four subjects. If assessment were to be restricted to a smaller ability band or if the numbers of subjects were to be increased, it is

Table 2.2: The percentage of pupils nominated as in the top ten per cent in only one, two, three or four subjects

No. of subjects	1	2	3	4
Teacher nomination	45%	23%	20%	12%
Test nomination	40%	30%	15%	15%

interesting to conjecture that *very* small numbers would appear in the cells indicating high ability on all or most subjects.

Our own focus, then, was on pupils with high ability in a specific academic subject and we would argue that this is of considerable relevance to secondary schools which still split up their curriculum along these lines. It is respectable to identify talent and enrich where necessary in a subject-specific way. Indeed there are implications that this should be done. The consequence is that instead of looking for a small elite of children with all-round ability we are encouraged to look for and develop the particular talents of each individual. A result of this approach is that a large number of children will enter the overall talent pool. The size of the combined 'gifted' group will, in the end, depend on the width of our definition of high ability. This, in turn, will depend on the width of our concern. For example, if we thought that the top ten per cent in each subject required some form of enrichment (and there is evidence, particularly from the extensive HMI surveys, to suggest that this may be so), then our tables would suggest that about 25 per cent of the school population would appear in the talent pool from the four subjects that we studied. We estimate that this would rise to perhaps 40 per cent over eight subjects, particularly if we were to include such subjects as art, sport and woodwork in our study. Such a size of talent pool would surely lay emphasis on the need for a large number of individual subject teachers confident in their identification strategies and strategies for provision for able pupils, first because of the large numbers involved, and second because of the subject-specific focus of both identification and provision, requiring subject-specific expertise.

Another important point, which will be taken up later but mentioned briefly now, is that if a child's abilities are to be recognized he or she must be given appropriate challenge within a subject. If, as is often the case, pupils are separated into ability groups according to perceived abilities in one direction (often after the administration of tests of ability, which more often than not are tests of general ability in one form or another, or after the administration of a limited number of subject-specific tests such as mathematics and English) then there is the danger that pupils will not be put into the appropriate educational environment in a subject in which they have high potential simply because they have lower ability in another direction.

Finally, before considering the characteristics of children with high ability in a particular subject, the reader might think it wise to reflect on the use of the word 'gifted'. We have discussed how the term 'gifted', because of its past association with high achievement in tests of general ability, has come to be misleading. For this reason, when we choose to refer more to high ability in a particular area of human endeavour than to high general ability it might be wise to avoid the ambiguity of the word. In our own work, for example, we chose to use the terms 'more able' and 'most able' instead.

Having argued for the respectability and relevance of a subject-specific focus in our work with highly able pupils, our next step is to discuss the likely characteristics of the children in our target group. An awareness of these characteristics would, we hope, assist teachers in the process of identification based on the limited day to day contact which they have with their classes.

Here again we suggest that there is considerable misunderstanding. As a first step in our discussion we can introduce some data acquired from our own work which puts a different perspective on these characteristics from that which is normally presented in pamphlets and books intended for the classroom teacher.

The distribution of high ability pupils within the school sample

An important characteristic of pupils with high ability is the way in which they are distributed across schools. In particular will they be found in a large number of schools, or will they be clustered together in certain schools only?

In the first year of our study approximately 2300 third year pupils in a representative sample of schools in one county were tested in such a way that measures of potential for four separate subjects could be derived. In the second year of the study approximately 1500 pupils were tested in the same way in a sample of the same schools. It was therefore possible to see whether the high ability pupils (as discovered by tests) tended to cluster in particular schools or whether they were distributed through the schools of this county. It was also interesting to see if the high ability pupils occurred in the same schools from year to year.

The important issue that should be considered in regard to this study is centred on the fact that teachers will generally judge children relative to their own school norms and experience some difficulty in making judgements relative to national norms. The consequence might be that some children who would rank high nationally are underestimated if it is thought that a particular school rarely if ever has a 'gifted child' in its population. If able children are more widely distributed across the schools, however, and if teachers are aware of this, then they can begin to think more confidently in terms of national rather than local norms when they are assessing their ablest pupils. The effect should be to raise the expectations that some teachers have for these children.

The result of this study, as it turned out, clearly favoured the hypothesis that pupils were distributed in a more or less random fashion across the county. Even when we studied the extremely small subgroup comprising the top 0.5 per cent in the sample *as a whole*, all of the schools had pupils of this ability in at least one of the subjects (and nearly half of the schools had such pupils in all four subjects) in one or other of the two years of the research. Table 2.3 shows the numbers of such pupils in each school for the two years of the research and Table 2.4 shows the numbers of pupils who were in the top two per cent over the two years.

The top two per cent on IQ score has often been taken as the 'gifted' group for whom fairly extensive additional or alternative provision is required. Therefore if we adopt a subject-specific model it is not unreasonable to look at the top two per cent in each subject. Table 2.4 shows quite clearly that these pupils are distributed among all the schools of our sample: all schools had a number of these pupils in all four subjects in one or other of the year groups. As we implied at the beginning of this section, this might seem a self-evident truth until we reflect on the point that teachers often have difficulty in deciding what characterizes a 'gifted' pupil in their

Table 2.3: No. of pupils in each school judged to be in the top 0.5% (on test score) of the county population in each of the two year groups for each of four subjects

School	English		French		Physics		Maths	
	Yr1	*Yr2*	*Yr1*	*Yr2*	*Yr1*	*Yr2*	*Yr1*	*Yr2*
00	0	3	0	1	2	4	1	5
01	4	N/A	1	N/A	3	N/A	2	N/A
02	0	N/A	2	N/A	0	N/A	1	N/A
03	0	1	0	0	0	1	0	1
04	1	0	0	0	2	2	1	0
05	1	2	1	0	0	0	0	0
06	1	N/A	0	N/A	2	N/A	3	N/A
07	0	0	2	0	0	0	0	0
08	0	3	1	1	1	1	1	2
09	4	0	1	0	3	1	2	4
10	2	3	2	0	4	1	2	2
11	0	0	2	0	0	2	0	0
12	0	0	0	0	0	1	0	1
Total	13	12	12	2	17	13	13	15

N/A indicates that a school was not part of the study for the second year of the project.

subject and whether they are likely to find these pupils in the school in which they teach. It is not uncommon for an experienced teacher to make a remark such as 'I have rarely if ever met a truly gifted pupil', or 'We don't have the sort of catchment area for very able pupils. Go to school X if you want to find a gifted pupil.'

The figures in Table 2.4 suggest that certainly in a county such as Oxfordshire, the characteristics of a 'gifted' child are those that we see in the top few pupils we have in our classes year by year in the majority of normal schools. Those who look for a shining halo or the performance of an unquestionable genius should realize that there may be much that appears 'ordinary' about these pupils, particularly when they are under-challenged by their day to day work. When a particular school appears to have 'gifted' pupils year after year in a certain subject area, often demonstrated by the quality of work that they do and by the range of aptitudes that they clearly display, we might conjecture that the differences between these pupils and the

Table 2.4:   No. of pupils in each school judged to be in the top 2% (on test score) of the county population in each of the two year groups for each of four subjects

School	English		French		Physics		Maths	
	Yr1	Yr2	Yr1	Yr2	Yr1	Yr2	Yr1	Yr2
00	1	5	2	3	4	11	4	10
01	7	N/A	2	N/A	7	N/A	4	N/A
02	4	N/A	2	N/A	4	N/A	4	N/A
03	0	3	0	1	0	1	1	3
04	4	1	4	2	8	4	5	3
05	5	7	4	4	1	0	4	0
06	8	N/A	7	N/A	8	N/A	7	N/A
07	1	1	5	1	3	1	3	4
08	3	7	5	4	7	4	9	8
09	9	1	8	1	6	2	5	9
10	6	4	3	2	3	3	4	3
11	1	2	3	1	0	2	0	4
12	1	4	1	0	2	1	1	2
Total	50	35	46	19	53	29	51	46

N/A indicates that a school was not part of the study for the second year of the project.

best pupils elsewhere who have not demonstrated these 'gifts' so strongly is a direct consequence of the difference in the educational stimulus in the environments where the children are taught.

This last point leads us to add a word of caution regarding the remaining discussion of the characteristics that children with high ability in a particular subject might display. We will amplify this word of caution later but the point is essentially that the able children in our study demonstrated these characteristics only when the work in which they were engaged was appropriately challenging.

Checklists

Having outlined where the pupils with high ability might be found, and having implied that they are likely to turn up in a large number of comprehensive schools, we can turn to the sorts of strengths that we might expect these children to possess. Many people have tried to construct lists of such characteristics in the hope that these 'checklists' might be a useful aid in the process of identification. Our own work contained a strand aimed at the evaluation of such an approach to identification. We will reserve the discussion of this work for a later chapter, using this one to reflect on the sorts of characteristics that should appear on such checklists. The reader will soon realize that our own search for appropriate items demonstrated this to be a difficult task. We discovered that the lists of characteristics that are readily available are not appropriate for a subject-specific approach to high ability, and will illustrate this point through one of the widely used checklists. We will go on to discuss the process by which appropriate lists could be compiled, giving our own checklists as specific examples.

The usual approach in constructing a checklist has been to look to research to provide evidence about pupil characteristics so that teachers could be encouraged to look for appropriate clues. This very reasonable approach has led to the production of many essentially similar checklists. Shields (1973) has listed several of these. A further example is the list devised by Laycock (1957) and quoted as recently as 1980 in the DES pamphlet (Hoyle and Wilks, 1980) for the guidance of teachers.

Gifted Pupils:

1   Possess superior powers of reasoning, of dealing with abstractions, of generalizing from specific facts, of understanding meanings, and of seeing into relationships.

2   Have great intellectual curiosity.

3   Learn easily and readily.

4   Have a wide range of interests.

5   Have a broad attention-span that enables them to concentrate on and persevere in solving problems and pursuing interests.

6   Are superior in the quantity and quality of vocabulary as compared with children of their own age.

7   Have ability to do effective work independently.

8   Have learned to read early (often well before school age).

9   Exhibit keen powers of observation.

10   Show initiative and originality in intellectual work.

11   Show alertness and quick response to new ideas.

12   Are able to memorize quickly.

13   Have great interest in the nature of man and the universe (problems of origins and destiny, etc).

14   Possess unusual imagination.

15   Follow complex directions easily.

16   Are rapid readers.

17   Have several hobbies.

18   Have reading interests which cover a wide range of subjects.

19   Make frequent and effective use of the library.

20   Are superior in mathematics, particularly in problem solving.

In the context of our subject-specific approach to identification, it is important to remember that insights to be gleaned from earlier research are insights into the characteristics of the *high IQ children* who were the subjects of that research. Thus the checklists generated on the basis of such insights will, in principle, be of dubious worth for the purposes of the study of children with high specific ability.

Freeman (1981) provides warning of another kind of problem which she argues is inherent in many of the general checklists that have emerged in recent years. She writes:

> Some educationalists prefer to avoid IQ tests by, for example, drawing up lists of characteristics. In time the lists grow to accommodate the inevitable exceptions until they become so all-embracing that they would describe almost any child. Unfortunately the lists have not been tested for their validity or predictive value.

A further problem arises from the nature of the items which make up the lists. Much of the research that gave rise to the items was not classroom-based. It is therefore possible that, valid though these items might be as correlates of high general ability, they may not actually be observable in the classroom situation. Clearly what can be observed of a child in a study which devotes all of its efforts to the observation of an individual may not be suitable for use in the classroom, where direct observation of one individual cannot be carried out so intensively. (Indeed the clues that may be observable in class and that might point to a child as having some important trait might be more appropriate checklist items than a broad statement of the trait itself.) Certainly the ease with which a teacher can complete a checklist will be important because, in a busy classroom, this will be only one aspect of what the teacher has to do. When teachers are confronted with a checklist on which the items are too obscure for easy observation they may well lose confidence in the instrument and revert to dependence on their mark book and their general impressions of the pupils so that the checklist, though it may actually be completed, may have only a very small role in forming the teacher's final opinion of a child.

Thus there would seem to be several problems in the use of general checklists for the guidance of teachers, especially in making subject-specific identifications. It is therefore encouraging to note that, as well as listing several general checklists, the booklet on identification recently produced by Schools Council Programme 4 (Clarke, 1981) also contains a strategy which teachers might use in compiling their own list for their own particular purpose (such as subject-specific identification). The method, which is called 'Up the Pole', is a systematic way by which a group of teachers can agree on what items they will include on their lists. The items that they consider for inclusion are, however, drawn simply from their own experience, so the lists will not necessarily contain items which are valid indicators of ability in a subject. The items will be relevant to certain activities within the subject but will be based only on subjective judgements which will themselves be limited by individual experiences of the teachers involved. These experiences may themselves reflect the teachers' limited aims in their subject teaching.

Checklists containing the sorts of items which might emerge through the 'Up the Pole' method have been used in science in the selection of pupils for special provision. The 'Cleveland' checklist reported in the Schools Council booklet (Clarke, 1981) contains a variety of such items but it would require considerable research to ascertain which of them were particularly relevant to science and which were equally relevant to other subjects. For example, one of the items 'Has a wide range of interests and/or several hobbies, reads and talks accordingly' is the kind of ability associated with the general checklists. Another, 'Possesses an unusual imagination', *could* be important for science, and could be demonstrated to be so by research, but the item may not necessarily be valid. It could be argued that an 'unusual' imagination could hinder a child in accepting some basic scientific principles and that, in consequence, though he may potentially be a creator of new ideas, he might not be able to acquire a sound basis of knowledge from which the new ideas could come. These particular items are included on the basis of a certain kind of reasoning and the point is that the reasoning may well be unsound.

Straker (1981), in her companion booklet dealing specifically with able mathematics pupils, approaches the identification strategy with caution, quoting a wide range of items from behavioural criteria applicable to able children in general to specific items relating to particular aptitudes within mathematics. The teacher is left with the task of extracting what seems appropriate. This reflects the current position of uncertainty as to what is necessary and sufficient for a checklist relevant to a subject such as mathematics. It may be that many of the items from these lists would be valid, and some will have been included as a result of careful research, but this is only conjecture.

These examples illustrate that whereas the general checklists contain quite well-researched items but reflect an IQ bias, the potentially more interesting subject-specific checklists often contain items of unproven validity. This unproven validity of individual items may not be a catastrophic problem if the checklist as a whole could be shown to be effective in guiding teachers to make valid judgements about pupils. However very few studies have been conducted into the overall effectiveness of any form of checklist. Renzulli, Hartman and Callahan (1971) provide a detailed report on attempts to validate the *Scale for Rating Behavioural Characteristics of Superior Students*. This scale (Renzulli and Hartman, 1971) is very well constructed on the basis of research and contains four subscales (Learning Characteristics, Motivational Characteristics, Creativity Characteristics and Leadership Characteristics). The authors showed that there were high correlations between ratings on these subscales and other objective measures of the relevant characteristic. Solomon (1979) also makes passing reference to the effectiveness of a checklist in improving teachers' ability to identify 'intellectually gifted fourth year junior pupils'. These studies are intriguing in that they provide some general support for the idea that checklists may be worthwhile.

At this point, however, we will continue to discuss only the nature of the individual checklist items, and will show the end product of our search for such items for subject-specific checklists. We will leave the issue of the overall effectiveness of these instruments in the identification process to a later chapter.

A scrutiny of these subject-specific checklists and a comparison with the general checklist above should focus the reader's attention on the sorts of characteristics that are relevant for subject-specific identification so that he or she can begin to be deflected from the less appropriate general criteria so strong in the literature. At the same time, because the checklists *define* what each subject is, we arrive at another focus of our concept of 'giftedness'. A child who, relative to his or her peers, shows outstanding abilities with regard to the subject-specific checklist items can be thought of as 'gifted' in that particular subject.

Of the four subjects in our study mathematics was the only one which produced a checklist based on items backed by research validation. The following list is due to V.A. Krutetskii (1976). He found that pupils with high mathematical potential display the following characteristics more strongly than their peers:

1. Obtaining mathematical information
   A. The ability for formalized perception of mathematical material, for grasping the formal structure of a problem.

2. Processing mathematical information
   A. The ability for logical thought in the sphere of quantitative and spatial relationships, number and letter symbols; the ability to think in mathematical symbols.
   B. The ability for rapid and broad generalization of mathematical objects, relations, and operations.
   C. The ability to curtail the process of mathematical reasoning and the system of corresponding operations; the ability to think in curtailed structures.

    D. Flexibility of mental processes in mathematical activity.
    E. Striving for clarity, simplicity, economy, and rationality of solutions.
    F. The ability for rapid and free reconstruction of the direction of a mental process, switching from a direct to a reverse train of thought (reversibility of the mental process in mathematical reasoning).

3. Retaining mathematical information
    A. Mathematical memory (generalized memory for mathematical relationships, type characteristics, schemes of arguments and proofs, methods of problem-solving, and principles of approach).

4. General synthetic component
    A. Mathematical cast of mind.

We then compiled the following checklist based on Krutetskii's list and our own background work. The aim of this version was to highlight mathematical abilities which were valid components of overall mathematical potential but which were also observable in the classroom. A validity check was carried out on each of these items. This was done by devising separate tests for each of the items which could be used with individual pupils. A group of pupils of high mathematical ability were compared with a group of moderate mathematical ability and were shown to achieve higher ratings on each of the aptitude categories.

Checklist of mathematical aptitudes

UNDERSTANDING OF INFORMATION

1. Able to understand the formal structure of a problem, seeing the relationship between the items of information even when there is a lot to assimilate.

2. Able to see when there's redundant information in a problem even when there is a lot to assimilate.

3. Able to see when there is not enough information in a problem and to see what information is needed for its solution even when there is a lot to assimilate.

PROCESSING OF INFORMATION

4. Able to suggest plausible ideas that might lead to the solution of a new sort of problem.

5. Able to follow the logic in a long mathematical proof.

6. Able to construct mathematical proofs:
   a) similar to ones already demonstrated;
   b) requiring different logic from that already demonstrated but on a familiar topic;
   c) on problems related to a new or unfamiliar topic.

7. Quick to see when a method of solution that has been applied to problems in one topic will solve problems of a similar nature in another:
   a) with help;
   b) independently.

8. Quick to see when examples of a mathematical result have a wider and more general application: focuses readily on these generalizations rather than on the particular examples.

9. Able to follow a logical explanation or proof when valid logical jumps are made that miss out or assume some of the intermediate steps of logic.

10. Displays an ability to make valid logical jumps when using mathematical reasoning accompanied by the ability to provide the intermediate steps.

11. When a method fails in a process of reasoning is able to try an alternative approach incorporating what has already been validly reasoned into the new structure:
    a) in following someone else's logic;
    b) in constructing a system of logic independently.

12. Is able, when possible, to give alternative methods of solving a problem.

13. Is critical of inelegant solutions and strives in his/her own work for the most elegant.

14. Is quick to notice an incorrect step of logic or an invalid conclusion.

15. Is not content unless he/she has complete understanding of a mathematical concept, method or process of logic.

16. Adapts readily from a direct to a reverse train of thought.

MATHEMATICAL MEMORY

17. Has a good memory for a method of solution. Remembers a proof by its logic rather than by rote learning.

18. Has a good long-term memory for techniques developed for a particular topic. Requires little or no revision to regain previous levels of competence.

GENERAL

19. Shows little mental fatigue even after intense concentration on difficult problems.

20. Is not content to leave an interesting problem unsolved, but keeps returning to it at odd moments until success is achieved.

21. Can perform any arithmetical computation accurately and with ease.

22. When attempting to solve new sorts of problems displays a strong tendency to interpret and solve the problem in:
    a) a spatial/geometric way; or
    b) an analytic/logical way.

The items on the second list are not all independent and the relationship between the items on the two lists is shown below.

Krutetskii's Aptitude	*Relevant Checklist Items*
1 A	1, 2, 3
2 A	4, 5, 6, 21, 22
2 B	7, 8
2 C	9, 10
2 D	11, 12, 19
2 E	13, 14, 15, 20
2 F	16
3 A	17, 18
4	22

The considerable amount of work that has gone into the evolution of just this one subject-specific checklist should not be under-estimated and it is clear that similar work is still to be done in other subjects.

For the other three subjects in our study, literature review and discussion with teachers produced the following checklists. We offer them as examples of what can be produced rather than as definitive versions, mainly because so much appropriate research is still to be done to isolate the components of ability in the subjects taught at school. There were, however, a number of key initiatives in England that have formed a solid background to the literature review for this part of the work. The APU work on language performance was a starting point for English and French. The work of the London Association for the Teaching of English (LATE) (1965) and of the Schools Council (Holbrook, 1961) provided more of the numerous reference points for English as did work such as that of Earnshaw (1974) at the Examination Boards. Pimsleur (1964) and Oskarrson (1975) were major starting points for the French checklist. The APU science reports, the science section of the HMI report on gifted pupils (HMI, 1977) and the work of Clarke and Cutland (1977) in connection with the Cleveland Project were major influences on the physics checklist. This point should be clearly understood: it was possible to draw on a large amount of background literature for each of the subjects and we would suggest that specialist teachers themselves could readily find a route through the appropriate literature in the search for reasonable checklist items. Our reservation about the final list of items is not so much concerned with whether or not the individual checklist items were plausible, but more with the lack of research evidence concerning the validity of the list of items as a whole.

One further point about these checklists is important. They were intended as *guides* for teachers, not as instruments that would be completed and then, through some system of marking, would lead *automatically* to the identification of the able pupils.

We had in mind that teachers would have a considerable amount of data available from their records of pupils' day-to-day work and from test and examination results. The checklist items were therefore designed to direct teachers' attention to pupil characteristics which may not be adequately reflected in this existing data; to extend the teachers' information about pupils, not to represent the sum total of that information.

AC–D

English checklist

WRITING

1. Technical control
   (a) Writes complex sentences / shows syntactical sophistication.
   (b) Manipulates punctuation to ensure intended meaning.

2. Reader awareness
   Provides adequate context/background information in own writing: conscious of needs of potential readers.

3. Able to adopt a variety of registers/styles as suitable.

4. Humour/irony
   Has a sense of humour. Able to make connections revealing ironies/absurdity of situation etc.

5. Vocabulary
   Uses extensive resources of words. Willing to experiment.

6. Originality
   Strives for fresh, inventive plots/situations in fictions.

7. Sympathetic imagination
   Able to imagine and write from a wide variety of viewpoints.

ORAL

8. High oral ability
   (a) *Talking*. Able to express ideas out loud in group or one to one discussions.
   (b) *Listening*. Listens and responds appropriately to what others say in group or one to one discussions.

READING

9. Comprehension
   (a) *Factual*. Able to extract, select, synthesise facts from a passage of writing.
   (b) *Meaning*. Sensitive to subtle or implied meanings.

10. Personal reading
    (a) *Enthusiasm.* Is a keen and voracious reader.
    (b) *Range.* Is willing to tackle a wide range of reading material.

11. Reading out loud
    Can read out loud spontaneously with appropriate sensitivity and intonation.

12. Critical judgement
    Advances beyond purely subjective judgements. Elaborates on own opinions by reference to text etc.

French checklist

1. ATTITUDE
   (a) Shows enthusiasm for the study of French. Perceives the subject as relevant to own future needs.
   (b) Shows active interest in learning about French way of life and the life of foreign countries in general.

2. AURAL/ORAL SKILLS
   (a) Able to discriminate between foreign sounds.
   (b) Able to articulate foreign sounds.

3. ORAL RESPONSE
   Alert oral response to questions in French (may be better than written).

4. CONTROL OVER SOUND/SYMBOL CORRESPONDENCE
   Pronunciation not perverted by written form of language.

5. SELF-CONFIDENCE
   Not embarrassed when speaking French. Enjoys trying out French sounds.

6. MEMORY
   Shows clear evidence of good memory.

7. MASTERY OF ENGLISH
   (a) Knowledgeable of essential grammar, e.g. parts of speech.
   (b) Alert to nuances in own language.

8. FLEXIBILITY
   (a) Can adapt to an entirely new set of rules and can think within them.
   (b) Does not try to impose English style or syntax on French sentences when writing compositions.

9. ABILITY TO PUT THE LANGUAGE TOGETHER
   Independently makes new connections out of isolated units of knowledge. Makes creative use of French structures.

Physics checklist

HANDLING APPARATUS
   1. Is able to use new apparatus with little guidance but is aware of his/her limitations and seeks help where necessary.
   2. Treats apparatus with appropriate respect.

MAKING OBSERVATIONS
   1. Makes observations without any form of guidance and can select the relevant from the non-relevant.
   2. Does experimental work with care and has feeling for the magnitude and consequence of any remaining error.

LOOKING FOR PATTERNS
   1. Attempts to incorporate new observations with previous ones into a pattern.

COMMUNICATING
   1. Chooses appropriate methods of recording results (diagrams, tables, graphs, descriptive writing).
   2. Is accurate in technical use of common words.

EXPLAINING AND PREDICTING
   1. Is persistent in seeking to generate explanations – mere

descriptions will not do. May provide several explanations and rank them in order of plausibility.
2. Seeks to make predictions but remains receptive to unexpected results.

TESTING IDEAS
1. Seeks to test ideas experimentally and will reformulate the problem if necessary in order to make this possible.
2. Can make decisions about which variables to control and which to investigate.

MATHEMATICS
1. Is accurate in manipulating numbers and symbols.
2. Does rough calculations with an appropriate accuracy.

CONCEPTS
1. Learns new concepts with ease.
2. Can apply appropriate concepts to new problems.

GENERAL
1. Can see the direction of an argument, anticipate its outcomes and grasp its implications.
2. Has scientific interests.
3. Relates school science to the world outside the lab. Is keen to know how things work.
4. Can detect flaws in the logic of an argument.

We would suggest that it is of the utmost importance to draw the reader's attention to the differences between these checklists and also between the subject-specific checklists and the general checklist. The subject-specific checklists – whether validated or not – clearly describe abilities related to particular fields of endeavour. The items taken together give one view of what we mean by a subject and hence indicate where we should focus our attention when looking for subject-specific abilities in children. The general checklist does no more than guide us towards rather vague characteristics which are insufficient, if used alone, for subject-specific identification. In the end we come to the very simple principle that the characteristics of a 'gifted' child are that he/she displays strengths beyond those of his or her peers in relation to the aptitudes that are associated with the sphere of human endeavour in which the pupil is considered to be 'gifted'.

Chapter 3

The Role Of Tests In The Identification Process

Introduction

When a school attempts to plan a system for identifying its able pupils the aim will be to choose, from the whole population of the school, the individual children who would benefit from whatever scheme of additional or alternative provision is to be organized. In achieving this aim the school will necessarily have to work with tight constraints in terms of the resources (both money and staff time) which might reasonably be diverted from other independent activities to this particular task.

In such circumstances it will be important to consider various alternative strategies of identification, to highlight the strengths and weaknesses of each and then to choose a strategy (or combination of strategies) which is most likely to achieve the desired outcome in a cost-effective manner.

There are two clear strategies that immediately become the focus of attention. One is based on the professional judgement of teachers and the other is based on the results pupils gained on tests chosen specifically for the purpose. It is, in a way, reassuring to those responsible for determining the optimum strategy to know that the contrast of 'clinical judgement' (such as that of the teacher) with 'actuarial judgement' (such as that based on test results) is a long-standing issue in the psychological literature dating back to Meehl (1954). The general thrust of this work is that clinical judgement was not superior to actuarial judgement. If we look specifically at studies of the gifted we find the same message, i.e. that teacher-based identification strategies were judged to be less successful than test-based strategies. The most notable work in this field on children in their early secondary school years was that of Pegnato and Birch (1959). They found that teachers were only 45 per cent effective and 27 per cent efficient at nominating their 'gifted pupils'[1]. With such a low level of success it is not surprising that the general recommendation was that test-based measures of ability should be used for the identification of children with high general ability.

  If we look closer at such studies, however, we are led to question the relevance of their results to the identification of pupils with high subject-specific ability. This indeed led us to our own study of teacher-based strategies. In the next chapter we will look more closely at the results of our study. However, in this chapter we will focus more on test-based schemes, and will attempt to highlight why they are attractive compared with teacher-based schemes. We will then go on to discuss their limitations. With these limitations in mind, we will argue that teacher-based assessments could well be reconsidered, particularly in the context of subject-specific identification strategies.

Test-based or teacher-based identifications?

When schools face the task of identifying children of high ability, because of the constraints of time and money they are likely to opt for a strategy which allows them to identify individuals from large

---

[1] Teachers were asked to nominate their 'gifted pupils' and the teachers' lists were compared with ranked lists of the same pupils based on IQ scores. The figures of 45 per cent efficiency and 27 per cent effectiveness are related to a cut-off point of 136 IQ. The authors discovered that a combination of group IQ test and achievement test could be 97 per cent efficient in the same context.
  We should define the two terms 'efficiency' and 'effectiveness' at this point. If we were to list in some way pupils who we thought to be gifted, we could make two kinds of errors. The first is the inclusion of inappropriate pupils. The second is the exclusion of appropriate pupils. The effectiveness is the percentage of gifted pupils that we nominated correctly, and is influenced by the second sort of error. The efficiency is the percentage of pupils on our list who were nominated correctly and is influenced by both sorts of error.

groups. They are not usually in a situation where a single individual can be tested or observed in isolation with few constraints on resources. Both teacher-based and test-based assessment schemes suffer because of this: teacher-based schemes will depend on the observations of individuals that are possible from within a busy classroom, and test-based schemes will depend on the information that can be extracted from the group tests rather than the more valid but more time-consuming individual tests.

The evidence relating to each individual's abilities in the school situation can be thought of as a series of clues on the basis of which decisions must be made. The school must therefore opt for those identification techniques that will give the most reliable evidence within the limits of available resources.

If it were thought that the teachers themselves could be effective observers and recorders of clues to ability as these emerged in their day to day interaction with pupils, strong support could be given to teacher-based identification strategies. A moment's reflection, however, leads us to suspect that the teacher might have too many difficulties to overcome for his or her contribution to the identification process to be reliable, particularly within the constraints of secondary school teaching. Factors such as class size and the burden of general administrative tasks, in addition to the tasks of working through a comprehensive subject syllabus with about 30 pupils when the pupils are seen for just a few short lessons each week, would all seem to inhibit the teacher's ability to observe and record effectively. In addition the validity of the clues to ability recorded can be suspect when the sorts of challenges given to the pupils are frequently of a routine nature. If we consider the kinds of subject-specific profiles that a comprehensive identification scheme should allow a teacher to build up for each child (examples are given in the previous chapter) we will quickly realize the limitations of the evidence that has come to be recorded in most teachers' mark-books – overall marks or grades, based on largely impressionistic marking methods. We realize also that this mark-book information is rarely supplemented by data that can be discovered and remembered if a teacher finds opportunities to talk and work with individual pupils both in and out of the classroom. These constraints, together with the pessimistic interpretation which has been placed on the limited amount of research evidence which has to date been available (particularly on the results obtained by Pegnato and Birch (1959) during their work in the USA at high school level[1]) would leave a teacher, or others who accept responsibility for the more able, very suspicious of teachers' abilities in the identification process. With this lack of confidence the teacher would begin to suspect that a number of factors might bias his or her judgement. These factors might include the sex of the pupils, pupils' motivation in doing work, pupils' neatness in written work, and the home background from which they come. (For a review see Postlethwaite, 1984.) With such uncertainty, particularly in situations where there has been little pupil-teacher contact, it is not surprising that alternative identification schemes are sought. Test-based schemes offer a simple alternative, so that quick and useable information can be assembled. We will return to our own evidence relating to the effectiveness of teacher-based nomination in the next chapter, and devote the rest of this one to a consideration of test-based procedures. A major part of the preliminary discussion will highlight their shortcomings.

Test-based procedures

It can be argued quite strongly that the 'labelling' given to pupils from test scores might stay with them and affect their own self-perceptions and their teachers' views of their ability for a long time thereafter. Such labels are therefore important. Any test is limited in both reliability and validity, which means that if it is administered to a large sample of pupils we can expect some pupils to be wrongly labelled (and can even forecast how many pupils will suffer this fate). Therefore, even if the use of testing procedures *is* accepted as more reliable and more valid than a teacher's estimate, we must accept that there *will be* a certain amount of error associated with the use of the tests.

---

[1] It is, in fact, arguable that the pessimistic viewpoint may have been expressed too strongly. For example, it is possible to consider just one section of the results of Pegnato and Birch and in so doing emerge with a stronger conclusion concerning test-based accuracy in identifying gifted pupils than is appropriate. 97 per cent efficiency was the result of a combined strategy. The use of group intelligence tests in isolation, when the gifted group was defined as having a Stanford-Binet IQ of 136+, produced a variety of results: an effectiveness ranging from 92 per cent to 22 per cent with corresponding efficiency between 19 per cent and 56 per cent depending on the group test cut-off IQ ranging from 115 to 130.

The key question of test reliability is a relatively simple one: if the tests are administered on two occasions to a group of children how highly do the scores correlate? It is a straightforward matter for the test designer to refine a test in such a way that it will achieve a respectable reliability level – say above 0.8.

The question of validity is much deeper, however, and should not be confused with the question of reliability. It is concerned with whether the test measures what we hoped it would measure. For example, if we were constrained by our resources to embark on a very limited testing programme we might choose to administer a reliable test of general ability. In using the test scores as a basis for ability judgements across the school curriculum we would have to consider how well a general ability test, such as an IQ test, measures mathematical ability or ability in art, or even one of the aptitudes which make up, say a maths or art profile. Before we can have a gauge of validity we must determine what it is that we are measuring by deciding what we *mean* by ability within a certain field of endeavour, such as mathematics or art. If we are not careful we will define the abilities as those which we can measure by existing or easily devised tests and then merely aim at improving the reliability of those tests. In so doing we restrict our perspective of what counts as ability in a subject and enter the closed circuit based on what our tests can measure – a narrow test-based definition of ability, reliably measured.

Defects in this structure will of course show up when the tests are found to lack predictive value at a later time when, perhaps, a wider definition of the subject becomes the focus of attention. For example, we might give eleven-year-olds a certain mathematics test and grade the pupils into ability groups. The test itself could well be a very reliable test whose content is mainly arithmetic; in fact the test may well be a valid measure of mathematical ability at age eleven when the content of the particular mathematics course is heavily biased towards arithmetic. We might be surprised to find that the pupils' test scores no longer appeared to separate accurately pupils of different ability at age thirteen. This could, however, arise if pupils' ability to work with mathematical generalizations had become an important component of both the mathematical experience and the mathematical growth of the pupils by that age. Thereafter the arithmetic scores might turn out to be poor predictors of mathematical attainment, say in public examinations at age sixteen, when a wide variety of abilities making up a comprehensive mathematical profile come to be tested. An important danger is that some pupils will have been misjudged and inappropriately challenged between age eleven and age sixteen because of the undue reliance on the test scores in the identification process. This example illustrates the problem which afflicts *any* test situation, to a lesser or greater extent. It indicates one among a number of problems associated with school testing programmes, particularly when comprehensive knowledge of individual subject-specific abilities (perhaps a dozen somewhat independent aptitudes for just one subject) is required for more able pupils, and particularly when the assessments are to be a basis for prediction of future performance. Not least among these problems is the time and expense involved in a comprehensive testing programme, so that it is not surprising and a little worrying when an optimum choice of tests is made within these constraints.

In this context it is not surprising that tests of intelligence have maintained their standing in the identification strategies of educationalists. First, such tests have been developed to a high degree of reliability, and second, measures associated with general intelligence have dominated as the criteria against which ability is to be judged. The attraction of a simple reliable ability test in a school with limited resources is hard to resist.

Nevertheless, the IQ scores that are generated in an identification exercise are likely to be misused and become increasingly misleading as the children grow older. If the IQ scores are taken as a once and for all measure of ability, no account will be taken of a child's intellectual growth in the abilities not tested by IQ measures or of the testing conditions that may have influenced an individual's performance (Vernon *et al.*, 1977). We are warned, too, of the effect of cultural and environmental factors on test scores (Freeman, 1979).

To take account of the factors that might influence children's test scores, tests should be administered every two years or so (Vernon *et al.*, 1977). Even when such action is taken to reduce error, however, we cannot escape from the fact that IQ scores are only related to a particular sort of ability. Tests of specific ability should be given to supplement the evidence that is provided by general ability measures.

Three further problems arise, however. First a multitude of tests would be required to make assessments of the multitude of specific abilities, which would make a comprehensive testing programme so long and costly as to be impracticable. Second, in many of the tests that are available the 'g' factor is so prominent that it obscures the other abilities that it was intended to measure (Vernon *et al.*, 1977). Third, many available tests are more tests of attainment than of ability. Tests of attainment assume a common educational experience of all who are to be tested (Freeman, 1979) and can therefore give misleading results, though we would be wise to remember that the best of these attainment tests minimize the error and have the advantage over general ability measures that they are subject-specific. We cannot deny that IQ tests, because of the large number of fields of human endeavour to which general intelligence relates, can provide some useful evidence for those who seek to identify abilities in others. Similarly, many of the growing number of tests of specific abilities will also provide important information. At best, however, they can provide only limited clues to ability, which will need to be confirmed and supplemented. When insufficient resources of time and money are available, limitations are more strongly felt, in that only a limited amount of testing is possible. We are thus led to the view that an appropriate use of tests is to use them as *one* diagnostic tool or as *part of* an initial screening procedure (Vernon *et al.*, 1977).

Having accepted that tests of one kind or another may have a part to play in a screening procedure, a school is faced with the task of administering them. The cost and time limitations for this would normally prohibit individual testing and allow for group testing only. We are warned of the additional errors that impose themselves on the results of such tests (Vernon *et al.*, 1977). The tests themselves are more limited in the kinds of challenge that can be given and are less reliable than individual tests. Interpretation of results, particularly with regard to norms of score distributions, must be done with care.

The implication, then, is that though tests may have a role to play in the identification process, this role is limited by test reliability and validity and by the sorts of abilities that particular tests can measure. This is particularly so with the group tests that a school would probably be forced to use. Though group tests are useful sources of information about a group as a whole, any deductions that we make about an individual pupil who has taken a group test must be treated with caution.

A further caution is worth noting in the context of able children (Freeman, 1979). This is that a large number of tests have been designed with the whole ability range in mind and have turned out to be least reliable at the top end of the mark scale.

What requires careful consideration, therefore, is what and where the source of extra information might be that should supplement or replace information that tests can provide in the identification process. The method that would be most reasonable for schools would be to rely on the day to day knowledge that a teacher has of his or her pupils. A subject teacher would have the closest contact with pupils, could be expected to have an awareness of subject-specific aptitudes and be able to observe strengths and weaknesses in each pupil.

It could be reasonably expected that a teacher would know the pupils as individuals on a wide and appropriate set of subject-specific criteria, and provide the sort of evidence that group tests cannot easily produce in a normal school. The fact that the teacher has the task of identifying the talents of each individual from within a group must not be underestimated, but it does, nevertheless, seem that a teacher *could* be the main source of appropriate knowledge in the identification process, being in the unique position to make judgements on the individual in relation to the rest of the group with whom he or she is taught.

Having started this section with doubts about the effectiveness of teacher-based identification strategies it is remarkable that we have reached a point where we are arguing for the reconsideration of such strategies. This comes after a reflection on the many limitations of test-based schemes. We might argue that these limitations should be accepted when it is considered that teacher-based schemes are prone to higher levels of error. If, however, we could demonstrate that teacher-based assessments are more effective in a subject-specific context than has been demonstrated in a general ability context, then our confidence might be increased to move away from a test-based scheme, at least in part.

It is important to note the extent to which British projects have already come to this conclusion. A City of Birmingham Education Committee working party (City of Birmingham, 1979) presented a very well argued case for relying on teachers in addition to (or in place of) tests. They stressed the need to see identification as a continuous process of re-assessment of childrens' needs and emphasized that, because of this, the teacher would always be a major component in the identification system. One can find support for this view in the work of Renzulli, Reis and Smith (1981) in America. They suggested a 'Revolving Door Model' which was based on the idea that giftedness was not something to be assessed once and for all, but rather that children should move into and out of any special programmes for the gifted as their own needs change in relation to their normal schoolwork. Renzulli and colleagues argued that the ordinary class teacher must be central to a system based upon this model. This fits into the view already stated that a battery of tests large enough to provide an adequate map of the full range of abilities is unlikely to be short enough to permit the frequent use that would be necessary if it was to form the basic identification instrument in a 'Revolving Door' system.

At this point the reader might wish to reconsider the important role that teachers might play in test-based assessments of the more able. The extent of the teacher's involvement must of course depend on the evidence concerning his or her effectiveness in a subject-specific context; however, for the time being we must leave conjecture in the air and will return to it in the next chapter, when our own results will provide the evidence that we require. For the present we will continue with the issue of tests.

Before examining specific examples of tests that we used for our own project we can assemble a short list of key issues that anyone who is in danger of putting undue weight on test-based identification schemes should consider.

Issues to be considered in relation to test programmes

If psychological tests are to be used as the sole means of identification of able children we must remember:

(a) Each test provides evidence on only a limited range of abilities.

(b) Often the general ability component of tests (g) is very high even when the test appears, on face value, to test a particular ability within a certain subject area.

(c) There are a considerable number of individual aptitudes

within each subject (a subject-specific profile) which should be tested so that a comprehensive mapping of each pupil's abilities in a subject can be carried out.

(d) All tests have error, particularly when used as a basis for prediction.

(e) Tests are expensive and so a limited budget can only afford a limited range of tests, thus restricting the scope of a testing programme.

(f) Individual testing is usually far too big a task for a school to contemplate.

(g) Group tests introduce considerable error and a limit is imposed on what can be tested.

(h) Testing programmes should not be once and for all affairs, but should be repeated periodically.

(i) Many tests are tests of attainment rather than aptitude.

(j) Misinterpretation of a test score and possible 'labelling' of a child with that score can lead to under/over estimation of ability and expectations, which can be matched with underperformance of the child.

(k) Many of the tests that are easily available to schools are least accurate at the top end of the mark scale.

Having drawn out the limitations of tests at length, we will now look at some of the ways in which tests could have an important contribution to work with the gifted.

Pointers to effective testing schemes

It would be unwise not to include the possibility of using test information alongside teacher judgements. We intend to return to this in the next chapter, when we will discuss how such a combination might be achieved most meaningfully, but there is one situation that we should mention at this point. Whether or not we are using tests or teachers as the main agent in the identification process, we can use one source of information to direct us to look again at the evidence from the other. When teachers and tests disagree it could be because the two sorts of judgement are based on different kinds of information, so that each may help the other to eliminate error of judgement. This is particularly useful when it has not been possible to accumulate teacher-based evidence of pupils' abilities because there has not been much teacher/pupil contact time. It must be re-emphasized that there is a danger in over-use of test-based evidence, however, and the safest direction to move might be to make teacher judgements the main source of data and give pupils with high test scores and low teacher ratings the benefit of the doubt until other clues to ability emerge from day to day interaction. A second important use of group tests is to draw conclusions about the comparability in general terms of groups (class or school groups) of pupils. This might help to increase our understanding of what we might expect from the group as a whole. Of course, we would have to use great caution in making assumptions about individuals from within the group.

We suggest that there are two meaningful approaches to a testing programme that could be used as a component of the identification process for very able pupils. Each would require that a comprehensive battery of tests be repeated at appropriate intervals. In making these suggestions, outlined below, we realize that we may be pioneering new territory: we are challenging education to construct hierarchies of aptitudes which grow upwards from the practical school curricula rather than resort to statistical extractions from conventional tests from 'outside' the curriculum.

First, it seems to be possible for an appropriate aptitude profile to be assembled separately for each subject. It must be said that at the time of writing much background research is needed to assemble these aptitude profiles and to determine the independent components of ability within each subject, as well as how these profiles overlap from subject to subject. We could be encouraged by the considerable research that was done in mathematics by V.A. Krutetskii (1976) and also by the kind of work that the Assessment of Performance Unit (APU) has done in a number of subjects. The potential that exists for the mapping and monitoring of profiles of subject-specific abilities as they develop could then be exploited, making subject-specific testing a real and meaningful activity. This must be a thought for the future, however, and the extent of the final testing programme might in the end be too large for most schools to contemplate.

The second possible approach relies on the understanding of the somewhat independent components of human abilities that is gradually emerging from psychological research. Guilford (1967), for example, proposed a model of the intellect with 120 different components. These components are much narrower than the ability required for a school subject. However, as such multi-dimensional models of the intellect become more refined, we might be able to discover appropriate combinations of the component abilities which would indicate potential for success in particular fields of human endeavour such as are defined by school subjects. This development might allow the development of a more economical testing procedure. Nevertheless, it too would be a comprehensive, costly and time consuming programme. An advantage might be that the same testing programme could be used for a large number of subjects, different combinations of the separate components of that programme being used to indicate potential for each subject.

This was the approach that we adopted in our own research programme as far as we were able. From available tests we selected a comprehensive battery from which we developed subject-specific measures of potential against which we were able to judge teacher nominations of more able pupils.

There are two reasons to describe these subject-specific measures of potential at this point. First, and indirectly in the context of this chapter, it will enable the reader to see just how the work was done so that when we quote results later the background has already been established. Second, important in the present context, by discussing the subject-specific tests of potential that were derived we can demonstrate by example some of the important points that were mentioned above. It is unlikely that testing schemes at present used in schools are as comprehensive as the battery used in this research, so that errors of test-based schemes used in schools are likely to be greater than the errors in the testing programme that we will now describe. Hence the points that will be made will be applicable with even greater force to school-based testing schemes.

Test-based predictors for attainment within a subject: a case study

ESTABLISHING THE PREDICTION EQUATIONS

A wide ranging set of tests of aptitude and attitude were given to all third-form pupils in the schools that cooperated with our research. Used separately the test scores provided useful information, but a means of combining appropriate test scores from the battery was developed so that an optimum combined test score which correlated more highly with subject-specific ability than any single scale could be produced for each subject. This relied on the statistical procedure called Multiple Regression Analysis which is best run on a computer. The computer is programmed to seek, from the test scores, the optimum combination of tests for predicting success according to a defined criterion. In our case we required the best 'prediction equation' to estimate, as accurately as possible from the pupils' scores on the individual test scales, the O-level scores that those pupils could be expected to gain two years later, based on the test scores that were entered into the equation. Different combinations of test scores were found to give the appropriate prediction equations for each of the subjects.

For the convenience of the reader we will list the test scales that were administered to our samples of pupils and the prediction equations that were derived from them. We will also describe the test scales themselves briefly at this point.

The Differential Aptitude (DAT) Tests had components as follows: *VR (Verbal Reasoning)*, measuring the ability to understand concepts framed in words; *NA (Numerical Ability)*, measuring the ability to understand numerical relationships and facility in handling numerical concepts, *VN*, the sum of the previous two scales, giving a measure of general scholastic aptitude such as is measured by IQ tests; *AR (Abstract Reasoning)*, a non-verbal measure of reasoning ability; *CSA (Clerical Speed and Accuracy)*, measuring the speed of response in a simple perceptual task; *MR (Mechanical Reasoning)*, measuring an understanding of mechanical and physical principles in familiar situations, these being presented in pictorial form; *SR (Space Relations)*, measuring the ability to visualise three-dimensional objects which could be constructed by folding the two-dimensional patterns shown in the questions; *SP (Spelling)*, a test of the student's ability to identify the correct spelling of familiar words; and *LU (Language Usage)*, measuring the ability to distinguish between good and bad grammar, punctuation and word usage. This battery tested a wide range of aptitudes that could be associated in differing amounts with the abilities required for the subjects in our study. The series of attitude tests contained eight different scales which measured children's views of their school, their class, their teachers and themselves as pupils. The tests of creativity followed the work of Torrance (1961) and contributed three scales that resulted from the pupils' responses to open ended tasks. The scales were *Fluency*, measuring the number of ideas produced, *Flexibility*, the number of different *kinds* of ideas produced, and *Originality*, the ability to produce novel or unusual ideas.

Similar 3rd year test data was available on two groups of pupils who had already gone on to take their O-level examinations in their respective 5th years in 1977 and 1978. It was from the test scores and subsequent O-level performance of these pupils that the prediction equations were established.

THE TEST BATTERY

Differential Aptitudes[1]	VR	Verbal Reasoning
	NA	Numerical Ability
	VN	VR + NA (General Scholastic Ability Scale)
	AR	Abstract Reasoning
	CSA	Clerical Speed and Accuracy
	MR	Mechanical Reasoning
	SR	Space Relations
	SP	Spelling
	LU	Language Usage
Attitudes[2]	A	Attitude to School
	B	Relationship with Teacher
	C	Academic Self Image
	D	Attitude to Class
	E	Social Adjustment
	F	Anxiety in Class
	G	Importance of Doing Well
	I	'Other' Image of Class
Creativity[3]	FLU	Fluency
	FLEX	Flexibility
	ORIG	Originality
Other Variables	SEX	Boy or Girl
	NT	Neatness[4]
	SC	Social Class

THE PREDICTION EQUATIONS

Subject	Equation for Calculating Predicted Score	% Variance	Standard Error	Best Single Predictor	% Variance
Eng	0.65 LU + 0.35 SP + 0.66 VR + 2.64 B + 31.26	36	15.18	LU	22
Fr (0120)	2.17 LU + 9.44 G − 7.18 A + 1.68 AR − 0.86 SR + 1.04 NA − 82.52	49	19.00	LU	28
Physics	1.45 MR + 0.54 NV[5] − 0.36 SP − 0.72 CSA +59.05	44	22.61	MR	25
Maths	2.66 NA + 0.72 MR + 1.53 AR − 6.6 E + 0.79 VR − 21.77	33	30.32	NA	21

NOTES

1. *5th Manual for the Differential Aptitude Tests* (Bennett, C.R., Seashore, H.C., Wesman, A.G.) Psychological Corporation 1974.
2. NFER SF7 scales. Attitudes to School.
3. NFER SF4 Free Writing Test.
4. The neatness mark was on a 1 to 5 scale and was assessed by the research officers who were able to standardize the scoring over the whole sample of pupils by giving a neatness score to their test papers.
5. NV = NA × VR.

Appendix 1 contains details of the work done in the formation of the prediction equations. Those readers who are interested may wish to consult the appendix at this point.

It must be remembered that the prediction equation is a way of combining scores to achieve a predicted O-level score that is as close as possible to the actual O-level score which the pupil will achieve in the future. Because we used the 'forward stepwise inclusion' procedure for our Multiple Regression Analysis (Nie *et al.*, 1975), the first variable in each equation can be interpreted as the best single predictor for O-level performance in that subject. However, it does not follow that out of all of the remaining variables, the others that are included will be the next best *single* predictors. Each variable that is entered is simply the variable which *adds* most to the variance explained by the variables already in the equation. Of two variables that are highly correlated with O-level mark and also highly correlated one with the other for the particular group of children under consideration, only one will appear in the equation as the amount of *extra* variance that would be explained by including the second variable would be negligible once the first one was in the equation. The variables included in the equation can each be assumed to make some independent contribution to performance in the subject and, between them, they account for as much variance as possible in the examination mark.

It is interesting to note that no creativity scores feature in the final equations and that, in general, the DAT scores account for most variance.

The standard error is an important measure, being the standard deviation of the difference between predicted and actual examination marks. The fact that in all subjects the standard error is substantial indicates the need for extreme caution in using knowledge of scores, even from this extensive battery of tests, completely to judge the potential of the pupils. The equations could, however, be used as a source of information to teachers in the identification process. If they are used in conjunction with other information – information about the pupils that is not entered into the equation – the predicted scores can be a useful piece of evidence of ability, but it would be extremely unwise to rank order pupils on their predicted scores and take no account of test error. The one or two marks that separate some pupils on this rank ordered list can be extremely misleading.

Another very important point is that the main predictors for the subjects are quite different from one another. This reinforces the view that identification of the more able in a subject-specific way is correct. None of the final equations is dominated by VN (which is a measure of general scholastic ability, correlating highly with IQ). In fact the variable which turned out to be the best single predictor in each subject (Language Usage in English and French, Mechanical Reasoning in Physics and Numerical Ability in mathematics) is the variable which one might have expected to fulfil this role. This adds a certain face validity to the equation. Together with other evidence, it also demonstrates the care which should be exercised in judging pupils' abilities *from subject to subject*. A child able in one subject is not necessarily so in another and, perhaps more importantly, the absence of high ability in one subject should not necessarily mean that ability is not present in another subject. This clearly has implications for the way in which we should establish streams and sets for teaching purposes.

To investigate the robustness of these prediction equations a check was made of the actual O-level examination results (released in confidence by the Oxford Examination Board and the Oxford and Cambridge Board) which came to be available two years after the first year group was studied. Table 3.1 shows the correlations and average errors of prediction when predicted and actual results are compared.

Table 3.1: Pearson product moment correlation coefficients between actual and predicted O-level scores (figures for comparison are shown in brackets)

	Correlation coefficient	(Estimate from multiple regression analysis)	No. of cases	Standard deviation of difference betweeen predicted and actual scores	(Standard error of pred.)
English	0.58	(0.6)	273	17.13	(15.18)
French	0.48	(0.7)	109	24.64	(19.00)
Physics	0.53	(0.66)	84	22.91	(22.61)
Maths	0.57	(0.6)	109	30.75	(30.32)

The evidence suggests that the prediction equations are robust. The slightly lower correlation between actual examination score and predicted score in French may have been a result of the very limited entry of pupils in this subject, but in the other subjects the correlation is convincingly close to the estimates. (The differences are not significant at the five per cent level.) The important comparison in all four subjects is that between the average actual error of prediction and the estimate (standard error of prediction). We see that these figures are very close in all subjects. We will see later that a knowledge of the average test error played an important role in our more searching statistical work. Furthermore, it is the average error that a teacher should have in mind when drawing conclusions about the relative abilities of two pupils who score similar but not identical marks as a result of a test.

We are now in a position to discuss some of the important issues mentioned earlier in the chapter, remembering that the tests we are discussing (that is, the overall subject specific test predictors) are likely to be better than those available to schools.

USING THE TEST SCORES

The list shown in Table 3.2 is illustrative of a ranked list of pupil scores – in this case a list of English scores that were actually obtained.

Suppose we are interested in identifying the top ten per cent based on O-level potential in the third form. The test ten per cent line separates pupils who differ by just 0.2 of a mark, yet the list of scores once neatly set out on paper could well lure us towards the view that they represent an accurate reflection of pupils' abilities. More importantly, when they represent the only evidence that is available or the only evidence to be used, the scores must be treated as if they were entirely accurate.

A score difference of 0.2 is of course meaningless in the context of an average predicted error of 15.2. We can illustrate the impact of the test error in the following way.

Suppose we divide the ranked list into three groups. The middle group (B group) is in a band from 0.675 × average test error below to 0.675 × average test error above the ten per cent line. In statistical terms the width of the band below and above the ten per cent line is called the *probable error*. Group A is then above this and group C is below. Group B then represents a group of pupils over whom there is considerable uncertainty. From our knowledge of the background distribution of scores, we can show that *at least 25 per cent of* the pupils below the ten per cent line and in the B group *can be expected to be in the top ten per cent group* when the actual O-level results emerge. This reflects the considerable uncertainty attached to test

Table 3.2: Illustration of the use of pupils' list rank ordered by the tests

	School 20 Name	Subject: English Predicted score
A group	pupil 1	125.2
	pupil 2	123.9
	pupil 3	122.6
B group	pupil 4	120.2
	pupil 5	119.3
	pupil 6	119.1
	pupil 7	116.2
	pupil 8	114.7
	pupil 9	113.5
	pupil 10	113.2
	pupil 11	112.9

--- 10% line

	pupil 12	112.7
	pupil 13	111.8
	. .	.
	. .	.
	. .	.
	. .	.
	pupil 21	108.6
C group	pupil 22	105.3
	pupil 23	105.1
	pupil 24	105.0
	. .	.
	. .	.
	. .	.
	. .	.
	pupil 93	63.4
	pupil 94	67.8

scores of pupils in this band and it is important to note that the greatest uncertainty is associated with the band closest to the ten per cent line – the band in which we would hope for the highest precision!

Similarly at least 25% who scored above the ten per cent line in the B group would not be in the top ten per cent at O-level. At least 75 per cent of those in the A group could be expected to remain above the ten per cent line at O-level, hence making this group a set of fairly confident test nominations. Similarly at least 75 per cent of C group nominations will not achieve a mark at O-level to put them into the top ten per cent group.

An area of uncertainty extends either side of our ten per cent group boundary. This will be so *whenever a test is used for the purpose of prediction*. We would suggest that the average error of prediction is far lower in the case of our carefully derived prediction equations than it is in most tests available to teachers, particularly if they require a cheap and easy to administer testing programme.

Furthermore, the average error of prediction is only an average and there will be some pupils for whom the error of prediction is much higher. If we had a very large list of pupils ranked according to their predicted scores we could subdivide the list into bands right through the ability range and make statements, such as were possible for the division into three bands that we made for a single year-group of one school, of how many pupils in each score band should really be nominated for the top ten per cent. This implies that right through the score range, even down to bands of very low scoring pupils, there will be a number of pupils who because of the error of the tests will be grossly misplaced by their test scores. We must remember too that we have considered subject-specific tests in the above discussion and we might conjecture that the degree of 'random' error will be much greater if the tests are inappropriate for the subject under consideration; for example, when judgements of abilities in a range of subjects are made on the basis of scores on a verbal reasoning test, when the degree of error varies from subject to subject. If we were to use test evidence alone there would be no way in which the misidentified pupils could be located – we would not know which of the pupils in each of the test score bands had been misplaced. Here we are reminded again of the danger of misplacing such pupils in ability sets as a result of test scores; there is the real possibility that they will underperform according to the level of challenge and expectation so that their potential will continue to be underestimated.

By focusing on the set of tests used in the research we hope to have illustrated some of the practical concerns and restrictions that are associated with testing programmes. Our tests were intended to be subject-specific and we can see from the large assortment of aptitudes, attitudes and other data available how different combinations of tests contributed to different prediction equations. We would add that if any one test (such as a general ability, verbal reasoning or numerical ability test) had been used then not only would the average error have been greater (building up a wider band of uncertainty either side of the cut off line for the top ability group) but also the same pupils would have been identified for all of the subjects.

In the next chapter we move on to discuss the effectiveness of teacher-based identification. Having first explored the limitations of tests, we hope that we can bring the importance of the role of teachers themselves into context. After exploring that issue in some detail, we will return briefly to how teachers and tests might be used together.

Chapter 4

The Effectiveness Of Teacher-Based Identification Of Pupils With High Ability

Introduction

So far we have outlined two main identification strategies: one based on teachers' judgements, the other based on test results, and have considered some of the advantages and drawbacks of each scheme. Certainly when one considers the pressure under which teachers operate and the range of tasks they must undertake it is clear that the opportunities available for them to work with pupils as individuals can be extremely limited and it is easy to see why test-based procedures might have considerable appeal.

However, it will be clear from the previous chapter that test-based procedures also have their limitations, especially when group tests are used as the sole means by which *individual* pupils are chosen from the whole school population for some form of further provision. This tempts us to look again at teacher-based procedures.

We have not put forward an optimistic viewpoint so far, but there are a number of reasons why teacher-based identification strategies could be at least as effective as tests. Opportunities for a teacher to gather clues to children's ability may be limited but the clues will be judged in the context of the stage of development children have reached and in the context of the schoolwork that they are doing. Furthermore, the clues can be assembled from day to day and week to week so that judgements can be refined as time goes on. The question remains as to whether such clues will allow identifications to be made with equal or less error than test-based schemes. The interesting point is that, with the uncertainties of testing procedures in mind, we might now ask this question with a more open mind.

We undertook to do this in our detailed fieldwork. It became a fascinating exercise to study the extent to which test-based lists of pupils overlapped with teacher-identified lists, and then to explore the implications of this overlap in more detail. Having set the scene in this way we would expect that the reader is beginning to speculate on the kinds of questions which one might ask and the answers which might emerge. To set some markers, and make the reading of the detailed findings easier, we will now summarize our main findings before moving on to present some of the background evidence.

Brief summary of the conclusions

(a) Teachers were found to be more accurate at identifying pupils of high ability in a subject-specific way than the work of previous researchers who were concerned with identification of general (IQ based) ability had suggested. This applied to all four subjects, maths, physics, English and French, but the effect was particularly marked for maths and English.

(b) When allowance was made for test error, a certain number of mismatches between teacher-based and test-based predictions could be expected without there being any implication that the teachers had definitely made errors. With these overall numbers of expected mismatches in mind, teacher-based identification in maths and English was found to be very successful. In physics and French, there were larger numbers of mismatches than could be expected solely in terms of test error, so although there were encouraging signs that the accuracy of identification by teachers was higher than had previously been thought, there was nevertheless evidence of some inaccuracy on the teacher's part in these two subjects.

(c) There were no large differences in the results for the different types of school in the study. In particular the schools catering for the 13+ age of entry showed similar levels of agreement between test-based and teacher-based identification to the 11+

age of entry schools – this despite the fact that our work focused on 13-year-old pupils.

(d) The ability of teachers to identify the top five and two per cents *as discrete groups* was lower in all subjects, but the percentage of these pupils who were included in the teachers' top ten per cent lists was encouragingly high.

We now move on to a more detailed discussion of these points. There were a number of components to the overall enquiry.

Preliminary investigation of the match between test- and teacher-based identification

In the last chapter we described a procedure for establishing test-based 'top ten per cent' groups of pupils in each subject area in each school. We have also drawn attention to the error associated with the tests and the consequent dangers of assuming that the pupils in these test-based groups are exactly those who should appear on the teachers' list of 'top ten per cent' pupils. There was, however, one useful purpose to be served in investigating the extent of agreement between these crude test-identified groups and teachers' lists: such investigations are broadly in line with the methodology used by Pegnato and Birch (1959) and by Solomon (1979) and so allow us to relate our work to theirs. However, it cannot be too strongly stressed that to use the test results in this simple way disregards the test error. This is a severe limitation of which the reader must be aware.

The identification was intended to be from the whole of the third form, not from any particular sub-group such as the top set in the subject. The results of the simple comparisons between the teacher-based and test-based groups are set out in Table 4.1.

When similar results were calculated for the sample as a whole, the figures shown in Table 4.2 were obtained.

The fact that the school which showed the closest match in English was also the school which showed the worst match in physics is a hint that the range of match between teacher-based and test-based judgement may be a reflection of teacher variation rather than of the impact of different school size, type or organization. This hint was confirmed by some of our later work.

Table 4.1: Percentage of test-identified pupils also identified by teachers (number in group is given in brackets)

School	English	French	Physics	Maths
00	57 (14)	69 (13)	44 (16)	64 (14)
01	67 (18)	52 (23)	43 (21)	59 (17)
02	53 (19)	58 (19)	52 (21)	65 (20)
03	75 (15)	50 (12)	50 (14)	36 (14)
04	67 (18)	25 (16)	20 (20)	53 (19)
05	56 (16)	62 (16)	53 (15)	78 (14)
06	70 (20)	50 (20)	48 (23)	50 (20)
07	50 (22)	38 (21)	37 (16)	67 (24)
08	75 (12)	50 (12)	17 (12)	58 (12)
09	71 (24)	62 (24)	54 (24)	67 (24)
10	67 (12)	73 (11)	75 (12)	50 (12)
11	55 (11)	45 (11)	20 (10)	64 (11)
12	33 (12)	25 (12)	58 (12)	64 (12)
13	51 (35)	47 (34)	53 (34)	59 (35)

NOTE   At third-year level, school 13 exists in three fairly distinct units in which independent identification of able pupils was carried out. These units are therefore analysed separately as schools 10, 11 and 12 in the above table.

It is interesting to compare these figures with the results obtained by Pegnato and Birch in their work with 12 to 14-year-old pupils in the junior division of a junior-senior high school in Pittsburgh, USA. They asked teachers to nominate children who were 'mentally gifted' and matched these nominations against those who scored 136 or more on an individually administered Stanford-Binet IQ test. They found that teachers identified 45 per cent of those who were above this IQ threshold.

We have already pointed out that judgements of teacher accuracy can only be made if due account is taken of test error. Any consideration of the comparisons made in this section must bear this in mind and what the findings suggest must be investigated in greater depth later. We think, however, that some useful points are worthy of discussion here and it will be seen that these points do not contradict those in the later more detailed study.

Table 4.2:   Overall percentages of test-identified pupils also identified by teachers

School	English	French	Physics	Maths
All schools	61 (213)	51 (210)	45 (216)	61 (215)
Range of %	33 – 75	25 – 73	17 – 75	36 – 78

First we should point out that the general 'feel' of the results, namely that teacher effectiveness was higher in mathematics and English than in physics and French, was borne out by our later more searching statistical work. Second it is clear even from these crude comparisons that some teachers can make successful and acceptably high subject-specific identifications of pupils with high ability, so that it would be unwise to assume that Pegnato and Birch's findings can be transferred to this more relevant task. The success levels achieved by some teachers (roughly 75 per cent agreement with test-based identification in all four subjects) are high enough to give us confidence to embark on further enquiries about teacher-based schemes of identification rather than to put such thoughts on one side because of a low success rate such as was evident in Pegnato and Birch's work.

Identification in English and mathematics showed greater match between teachers and tests than was the case in physics and French. This may of course reflect greater inaccuracy in the physics and French *test-based* identification. However, evidence provided by the statistics associated with the regression equations which generated the test identified groups (especially the percentage variance explained – 36 per cent in English, 49 per cent in French, 44 per cent in physics and 33 per cent in mathematics – and the standard error of the predicted score – 15 in English, 19 in French, 23 in physics and 30 in maths) did not support this view. The equations in physics and French explained more variance in O-level score (i.e. gave predicted scores which were more highly correlated with actual O-level scores) than did the equation in mathematics and also resulted in lower standard errors. The physics and French equations also explained more variance than the English equation though admittedly, in this case, the standard errors were higher.

On forms issued to them, teachers were asked to identify 'that ten per cent of third-year pupils whom you expect to have the greatest potential for further work in your subject' and it could be argued that, in French and physics, potential for O-level performance does not coincide with this specification. While we would stress the important point that in discussion with the teachers it was clear that O-level potential *was* firmly in their minds, it *could* be that physics and French teachers tried to take account of other aspects of high ability. This difference in emphasis could contribute to the greater mismatch between tests and teachers in these subjects. We feel that the force of this argument is attenuated by the fact that in English, the subject where that which constitutes potential for further work in the subject might be expected to be furthest removed from that which leads to success in O-level English Language, the teachers and tests were in substantial agreement. We feel too that, with physics in particular, the nature of the subject makes it difficult to sustain the view that a third-year pupil could have potential for further work without having potential for O-level success. We should also point out that Murphy (1981) and Massey (1978) had already established high correlations between O-level and A-level performance in physics. This suggests that even if teachers were looking beyond O-level the pupils they picked should still be the high O-level scorers.

It would seem, therefore, that the greater mismatch between test and teacher judgements in French and physics may indicate a genuinely greater difficulty for teachers in making judgements about pupils in these subjects. This view was supported by the work on the characteristics of the teacher-selected groups which is discussed in a later chapter. Reasons for this difficulty would seem to be:

(i)   The difficulty of making accurate assessments of individuals' work in class (oral work in French, practical work in physics);

(ii)   the nature of the syllabus content in the first years (e.g. in physics little challenging mathematical work is usually undertaken below Year 4 so that pupils have little opportunity to display ability of this type);

(iii)   the small amount of teacher contact with classes (especially in physics where only an hour or so is spent in each class each week). This difficulty is compounded by the consequently large number of classes that the teacher has to try to get to know;

(iv)   the fact that, at the beginning of the third year, the work in physics (and to a lesser extent French) is at a fairly simple level because the subject is fairly new to the pupil. In maths and English, which have five primary years to build on, the work is beginning to get more challenging, and is more likely to provide opportunities through which the more able can demonstrate their ability.

School differences

DIFFERENCES BETWEEN INDIVIDUAL SCHOOLS

Table 4.1 indicates that, within each subject, schools seemed to vary in the extent to which teachers' and tests' judgements agree. To explore the question of whether or not these differences were too large to be attributable to chance, the data were cast into the form shown in Table 4.3 and analysed by means of the chi-squared test.

Similar analyses in the other subject areas are reported in Table 4.4 and lead to the conclusion that there were no statistically significant differences between individual schools in the numbers of test-identified pupils who were also identified by teachers.

DIFFERENCES BETWEEN 11+ ENTRY AND 13+ ENTRY SCHOOLS

Schools were grouped according to whether they accepted pupils at age 11 or age 13. Tables 4.5 and 4.6 show the results of comparisons between these groups.

The chi-squared values shown in Table 4.6 were calculated in the same way as that shown in Table 4.5 and were corrected for continuity (Seigel, 1956). The percentage figures are quoted to give an indication of the nature of the differences under investigation in the chi-squared analysis. The overall, and perhaps surprising, conclusion is that there were no statistically significant differences between the 11+ entry and 13+ entry schools. Even more surprising is the fact that the trend indicated by the results was that the *13+ entry* schools showed greatest agreement between test and teacher judgement. Several heads of 11+ entry schools suggested to us that this result may reflect the fact that there is often a substantial

Table 4.3: Teacher/test agreement: differences between schools in English

| School | Test-identified pupils | |
	identified by teachers	missed by teachers
00	8	6
01	12	6
02	10	9
03	10	5
04	12	6
05	9	7
06	14	6
07	11	11
08	9	3
09	17	7
13	18	17

$$\chi^2 = 6.60$$
$$df = 10$$
not significant (ns)

Table 4.4: Teacher/test agreement: summary of differences between schools

	English	French	Physics	Maths
χ^2	6.60	10.17	12.14	7.95
df	10	10	10	10
Significance	ns	ns	ns	ns

change of staffing between 2nd and 3rd year classes so that the additional opportunities for staff to get to know pupils in an 11+ entry school are more illusory than real.

An alternative suggestion is that, in 13+ entry schools, the first term of the school year is naturally a time when staff are attempting

Table 4.5: Comparison of teacher-test agreement between 11+ entry and 13+ entry schools in English

	Test-identified pupils		
	identified by teachers	not identified by teachers	% of test identified pupils also identified by teachers
11+ entry	94	60	61
13+ entry	36	23	61

$$\chi^2 = 0.024$$
$$df = 1$$
$$ns$$

Table 4.6: Summary of differences between 11+ entry and 13+ entry schools

Subject	χ^2 (df = 1)	% of test identified pupils also identified by teachers in schools with	
		11+ entry	13+ entry
English	0.02 ns	61	61
French	2.79 ns	47	61
Physics	2.18 ns	41	53
Maths	2.17 ns	57	69

to assess the new 3rd year intake, whereas in 11+ entry schools assessment of this year group at this stage of the year is a less pressing priority. It may be that the lower degree of match between teacher and test judgement in 11+ schools was a consequence of this fact: namely that the exercise was, for the staff of these schools, more artificial.

EFFECTS OF SCHOOL SIZE

For this analysis the 11+ entry schools were grouped according to size. School 13 formed a 'group' of its own with 2000+ pupils. Schools 03 and 08 formed a group of 'small schools' with fewer than 1000 pupils. Schools 00, 01, 04, 06 and 07 formed a group of middle sized schools (1000 to 1500 pupils).

The analysis of school size difference was conducted in a similar fashion to that reported in the preceding section and the summary table is given below.

Table 4.7:   Summary table of school size differences

Subject	χ^2 value (df = 2)	% of test identified pupils also identified by teachers		
		large	medium	small
English	2.38 ns	51	62	70
French	0.11 ns	47	46	50
Physics	2.68 ns	53	38	34
Maths	1.41 ns	59	58	46

No statistically significant differences were detected and no clear trends were discernible in the data from this aspect of the work. It should however be remembered that the large school (School 13) did function as three more or less independent smaller units. The possibility therefore remains that in a large school functioning as a single unit teacher-based identification may be differently matched to test-based identification.

These results taken together provide support for the hint to which we drew attention earlier: namely that variation was not dependent on gross organizational matters such as size or type of school but that it probably reflected variation in the effectiveness of individual teachers.

Comparison of teacher nomination with test prediction when test error is taken into account

We now move on to what we feel is a more important aspect of the analysis, in which we have attempted to take account of test error when comparing the teacher-generated nominations for the top ten per cent group with those arising from the tests. We have made this more meaningful comparison in two different ways.

It will be remembered that the ordered lists were divided into three groups: Group A containing those pupils who, even with test error in mind, scored high enough to rank them as very strong candidates for membership of the top ten per cent group, Group B containing pupils who scored high enough to be reasonable choices for the top ten per cent group and Group C containing the remainder of pupils, all of whom scored so low that even with test error in mind they were weak candidates for inclusion in the ten per cent group. The first comparison was based on the distribution of teachers' nominations across these three groups. In the second comparison we used a knowledge of the magnitude of the test error to calculate the total numbers of pupils in various bands of test score whom we could expect, because of test error *alone*, to be identified by teacher and not by test or by test and not by teacher. In this way we can judge if the level of mismatch is beyond reasonable expectation for each subject. If this had proved to be the case we could argue that there is evidence for error on the part of the teacher as well as the test.

The match between teacher and test judgements in terms of groups A, B and C

If we make allowance for test error, we are admitting to the inaccuracy of the test in predicting the potential of children for future O-level performance. However, almost paradoxically, once we have begun to take account of test error we can also begin to interpret differences between test- and teacher-based nominations not just as signs of disagreement between these two methods of identification, but actually as signs of error on the part of the teacher. In the simple work reported in Table 4.1 we knew that there was some disagreement between test and teacher nomination. As we knew that there was error in the test we could not imply that this disagreement was necessarily a sign of teacher error. However, as we begin to quantify the test error we can begin to make comments on the accuracy of teachers' judgements. For example, we know that *even in the light of test error*, at least 75 per cent of the pupils in the A Group will score well enough on O-level to be members of the top 10 per cent (though we are not able to tell from the tests which of the A Group pupils will achieve this). If therefore teachers overlook, say, 60 per cent of the A Group, then there is not only evidence of disagreement between teacher and test, but also fairly firm evidence that the teacher has made an error.

For the sake of clarity we can introduce a further classification in which the pupils are divided into groups that we will call 'Good', 'Satisfactory' and 'Unlikely' teacher nominations. This is illustrated in Table 4.8 which represents a list of pupils ranked according to their predicted score.

In terms of Table 4.8, Pupils 1 to 5 were the 'good' candidates for inclusion in the ten per cent group, being above the test top ten per cent line. Pupils 6 and 7 were 'satisfactory' candidates, being below the ten per cent line but above the lower 'probable error line', and pupils 8 and 9 et cetera were 'unlikely' candidates, being below the lower 'probable error line'. The spread of teacher nominations across these three groups will now be considered.

The figures in the final column of Table 4.9 reinforce the view that identification in French and physics showed the greatest mismatch between teacher and test judgements. We must consider the percentages in the third column – the percentage of 'unlikely candidates' for the top ten per cent group – in relation to the estimated percentage of pupils who could be expected to be low scorers on the test but who nevertheless because of test error could be perfectly reasonable nominations for the top ten per cent. Of a group of children at the top end of the C group we would expect (from a large sample) only some 25 per cent to be misplaced because of test error. We would expect less pupils to be misplaced further down the C group. Overall the figures of 12 per cent in English and 16 per cent in mathematics would seem to be roughly in line with this forecast, but the higher percentages of 36 per cent in French and 30 per cent in physics would provide us with evidence of considerable error of judgement in these two subjects. Of course these figures can be presented in an alternative way: if a large proportion of the 30 per cent of physics nominations are, in the sense

Table 4.8

	Pupil 1	*Group A*	More than a 75%+ chance of being 'above the 10% line'
	Pupil 2		
Good candidates for membership of 10% group			*Higher prob. error line*
	Pupil 3		
	Pupil 4		
	Pupil 5		
		Group B	
			10% group borderline
Satisfactory candidates	Pupil 6		
	Pupil 7		
			Lower prob. error line
	Pupil 8		
Unlikely candidates	Pupil 9	*Group C*	More than a 75% chance of being 'below the 10% line'
	.		
	.		
	.		
	.		
	.		
	.		

set out above, likely errors, 70 per cent can be thought of as perfectly reasonable nominations. In a similar way we can report that 88 per cent of nominations in English, 64 per cent in French and 84 per cent in mathematics were reasonable nominations. This implies that though we have evidence of error in at least two of the subjects in our study, there is also evidence of a relatively high level of success in teachers' nominations of pupils with high ability, in all four subjects.

Reported in this way the situation looks rather different from, and much more encouraging than, that inferred from the work of Pegnato and Birch. However, two important questions remain. First, what was it about the unlikely pupils which led teachers to nominate them as members of the ten per cent group? Second, what

Table 4.9: Percentage of teacher nominations falling in the three groups 'Good', 'Satisfactory' and 'Unlikely'

| SUBJECT | n | PERCENTAGE OF TEACHER NOMINATIONS WHO WERE | | |
		Good candidates	Satisfactory candidates	Unlikely candidates
English	213	61	27	12
French	210	51	13	36
Physics	214	45	25	30
Maths	225	61	23	16

is it about the reasonable nominations which *were* made, which set them apart, in teachers' minds, from the other equally reasonable pupils who were not nominated? This important point will be considered in a later chapter. Before looking more closely at the A and C groups we turn to the question of whether school size, or the age of the main intake, affected the distribution of teachers' nominations across the three categories (good, satisfactory and unlikely candidates for ten per cent group membership). Table 4.11 gives the full table of figures for all schools for physics which was subjected to the chi-squared test. Table 4.10 summarizes the results for all four subjects which were analysed in the same way.

Table 4.10: Analysis of individual school differences (sections of school 13 analysed separately)

Subject	Chi-squared values df = 24
English	20.2 ns
French	31.4 ns
Physics	43.1 1%
Maths	16.5 ns

Table 4.11:   Physics nominations: school differences

	NUMBER OF NOMINATIONS WHICH WERE OF		
School	Good candidates	Satisfactory candidates	Unlikely candidates
00	7	5	4
01	9	8	4
02	11	2	8
03	7	3	4
04	4	5	11
05	8	2	5
06	11	6	6
07	6	2	8
08	2	7	3
09	13	7	2
10	9	0	3
11	2	6	2
12	7	1	4

In physics but in no other subject a statistically significant difference was found between the schools treated individually. It seems from the chi-squared table that, in physics, school 04 nominated more unlikely pupils than expected whereas school 09 nominated more good and satisfactory pupils than expected. No explanations come to mind for this difference other than the simple one: that teachers vary in their ability to identify able children.

In all four subjects we found that there were no statistically significant differences between the 11+ entry and 13+ entry schools. Within the 11+ entry group schools of different size again showed no significant difference in the way their nominations were distributed.

The level of mismatch in groups A and C

We recall that the A group contained those pupils who, even when test error was taken into account, are likely to have an O-level score sufficiently high to confirm their membership of the top ten per cent and the C group contained pupils who in the same sense were unlikely to obtain membership of the top ten per cent. We can therefore consider the level of mismatch between test and teacher nomination within these two groups and make some preliminary judgements about the accuracy of the teachers' judgements. If teachers were making completely accurate identifications we would expect few mismatches in these groups.

Table 4.12 shows, for all schools together, the percentage of pupils in the A Group who were nominated by teachers.

Table 4.12: Percentage of 'A' group pupils nominated by teachers

	English	French	Physics	Maths
All schools	80.8	61.4	53.7	76.2

Analysis of the data which generated the results in Table 4.12 was undertaken to establish whether there were differences and between individual schools, between schools with 11+ and 13+ intakes, between schools of different size. Both the analysis to investigate individual school differences and that to investigate the effect of size were hampered by the fact that very small numbers were involved. However the results of these analyses (treated with caution because of the problem of small numbers) did appear to indicate that there were no significant differences.

The analyses of schools grouped by age of entry did not suffer from small number problems and, in common with earlier results of a similar kind, no significant differences were detected.

It is perhaps surprising that after half a term's knowledge of the pupils, teachers in all schools should overlook between one fifth (in English) and almost one half (in physics) of those pupils who, on the tests, fell into this high-scoring 'A group' category. We must remember, however, that in all score bands we do expect some test-teacher mismatch because of test error. This can be as high as 25 per cent of the pupils whose test scores placed them on the boundary of this group. In view of the definition of the A group, therefore, while the English result does not force us to the assumption that errors were made by the teachers, the physics result does strongly suggest that this was the case.

Table 4.13 shows, for all schools together, the percentage of pupils nominated by teachers who were in the C group.

Table 4.13: Percentage of teacher selected pupils who were in the C group

	English	French	Physics	Maths
All schools	12.2	35.7	30.4	15.8

As in the A group analysis we found no indication of individual school differences in the extent to which teachers' nominations fell into the C groups. We also found no indication of differences between schools grouped according to size. Again as in the A group analysis, small number problems rendered the chi-squared tests used to establish these results rather suspect. However, the analysis of schools grouped according to age of intake avoided small number problems and again failed to disclose any significant differences.

Consideration of the results indicated to us the greater accuracy in English and mathematics compared with French and physics and led us to the analysis that will now be described.

When school data were pooled we obtained a much larger sample of pupils than could be derived from any single school. This enabled us to do some more detailed statistical work in our search for evidence concerning teacher effectiveness in the identification process. For schools separately it was possible to divide the ranked test list into three groups (A, B, C) and estimate how many pupils, in the light of test error, could be expected to be mismatches with regard to teacher and test nomination if teachers were correct in their judgements. Only three groups were advisable for this analysis if comparisons involving very small numbers were to be avoided, but the C group itself was rather large – about 85 per cent of the year group. The tests would provide more errors near the boundary of this group, however, than further down the list, so that a considerable number of test/teacher mismatches low down the C group could be considered as evidence in support of actual teacher error. With the pooled sample of pupils it was possible to divide the ranked lists into narrower score bands, estimate how many teacher/test mismatches we would expect in each band if teachers had made no errors and see if there was any statistically significant difference between the numbers of pupils selected in our study. A similar division into a number of narrow score bands was possible above the ten per cent test line so that we could detect whether a significant number of high scorers were being missed by teachers.

It was encouraging in both English and maths that the *number* of mismatches between teacher and test predictions in all of the bands of scores corresponded to the number which might have been expected as a result of test error alone. We must, of course, point out that even if numbers correspond, the particular pupils may not.

In the case of French, even allowing for test error, there was still a significant difference between the numbers of pupils who may be expected to score differently from their predicted scores and the number of high scorers missed, or low scorers selected by teachers. It would appear that too many low potential pupils are being assessed among the top ten per cent and far too many highly able are being missed. In physics there was a similar if not quite so marked discrepancy. It is interesting to note that in both subjects the discrepancy was noticeable among pupils whose score was more than half a standard error either side of the 90th percentile score and became more acute in the extremes of the score ranges. These areas of worry correspond roughly to the A and C groups of our main analysis.

We are therefore led to believe that, in physics and French, the *numbers* of pupils missed from the A group or selected from the C group *do* represent teacher error. In English and maths the number of mismatches is in line with what as a consequence of test error may be considered reasonable.

A useful alternative interpretation of these results is that in English and mathematics we found evidence to support the view that the accuracy of teacher judgement is equal to that based on test prediction. We will take up this point a little later when we look at the results that were obtained by the pupils who went on to sit their O-level examinations. Before that we will look briefly at smaller subgroups of the top ten per cent.

Subsets of the top ten per cent (top five per cent, two per cent etc.)

If we use the same categories of 'good', 'satisfactory' and 'unlikely' classifications for teacher nominations with regard to a line drawn under the top five per cent on the ranked test list of pupils, using the same measure of 0.675 × standard error to determine the band of probable test error below the five per cent line in which the 'satisfactory' teacher nominations fall, we arrive at the percentages in the table below.

Table 4.14: Percentage of teacher nominations falling in the three groups 'Good', 'Satisfactory' and 'Unlikely' (top five per cent)

		PERCENTAGE OF TEACHER NOMINATIONS WHO WERE		
Subject	n	Good candidates	Satisfactory candidates	Unlikely candidates
		for the top five per cent		
English	101	53	27	20
French	101	37	22	41
Physics	81	35	26	39
Maths	96	48	31	21

We see that the level of success appears to be a little lower than in the situation where teachers were asked to nominate the top ten per cent. There is, therefore, increased concern about teachers' ability to nominate the top five per cent group accurately. This was particularly so in physics and French, and by implication in other subjects where a teacher's classroom contact with pupils has been restricted. The proportion of unlikely nominations is still not at a critical level (in particular it is still of the order of only 20 per cent in English and mathematics). We might optimistically conjecture that there may be ways in which teachers could be trained away from the sorts of biases that affect their judgements rather than recommend strategies based only on testing procedures.

There is an important trend in these figures, in that teacher accuracy appears to decrease by the order of five to ten per cent when the teachers are asked to nominate the top five per cent rather than the top ten per cent. If we conjecture how this might extrapolate to smaller subsets of the more able group, we arrive at a view that we might not have forecast, namely that teachers find more, not less, difficulty in the identification of the most able pupils.

The conclusions reached for the A group extend our evidence in this direction when we consider the percentages of pupils that these groups represent (3.4 per cent in English, 3.8 per cent in French, 3 per cent in physics and 2.7 per cent in mathematics).

By counting, as successful nominations for the A group, those pupils who were nominated for the top *five* per cent by their teachers and whose test score placed them above the A group probable error line, we arrive at the following estimates of effectiveness and efficiency for this approach to teacher nomination of the top two to three per cent. We would stress that these are *estimates*, but in view of our findings we feel that they are realistic.

Table 4.15: Estimates of effectiveness and efficiency of teacher nominations for the top two to three per cent (based on nomination for top five per cent)

	Effectiveness	Efficiency
English	100	68
French	68	52
Physics	87	52
Mathematics	100	54

Although this does not change our point of view, which is that the success level would be lower if we had asked teachers to nominate the top two to three per cent directly, we see that if we are willing to widen our teacher-based lists (for example to the top five per cent in order to nominate the top two per cent successfully) we can achieve a high level of success in nominating the smaller subgroups of the top ability sets without recourse to very low efficiencies. It is important to note, in this context, that teachers were far happier to attempt to identify the top five per cent than the smaller subgroups such as the top two per cent, so that the above table shows meaningful results for the practical situation. Since our optimistic estimate was of 100 per cent effectiveness for English and mathematics we conjecture that a higher efficiency might be possible if we asked teachers to attempt to nominate a smaller subgroup than the top five per cent (say the top four per cent). These estimates were seen to be quite plausible when a limited study was carried out of the pupils who went on to take their O-level examinations two years later. If we had extended the teachers' lists to include the top ten per cent we would have estimated 100 per cent success in nominating the top two per cent in all four subjects and also 100 per cent success in nominating the top five per cent in all four subjects (with, of course, reduced efficiency levels).

Finally, we can reinforce our evidence as to the effectiveness of teacher-based identification of the more able by adding some brief comments about the limited study carried out on the actual O-level scores of a sample of pupils who were part of our initial study and went on to sit their O-level examinations two years later.

By pooling the results from all of the schools on which we could obtain data and then finding the grade levels attained by the top ten per cent and the top five per cent of this sample we were able to make a study of teacher-effectiveness of identification at third form level based on the pupils' *actual* exam performance.

The use of *actual* exam results allowed us also to assess the effectiveness and efficiency of our test-based *predictors* of O-level performance. We suggest that the top five per cent could be expected to gain an A or be in the top quarter of the B grade. Similarly the top ten per cent could be expected to gain an A or any B. It is difficult, because of the limited entries (particularly in French), for us to be exact when deriving the cut-off points in these subjects but we believe them to be reasonable criteria, especially since their major use is to provide a comparison between teachers and tests rather than to provide an absolute measure. Similarly we judged pupils who went on to achieve below a grade C to have been inappropriate nominations for the ten per cent group and those who attained below a B to be inappropriate nominations for the five per cent groups. Tables 4.16 and 4.17 show the percentages that emerged for each subject from this study.

For English and mathematics, a number of the most able were entered for earlier examinations and so did not enter into this analysis. We therefore suggest that for these two subjects the level of

Table 4.16: Overall percentage of pupils who were nominated for the top ability groups by teachers and who achieved the expected O-level grade

	English	French	Physics	Maths
Nominated for the top 10% and gaining an A or B	83%	74%	61%	75%
Nominated for the top 5% and gaining an A or top B	63%	68%	58%	62%

Table 4.17: Overall percentage of pupils who were nominated for the top ability groups by teachers and who achieved lower than the expected grade

	English	French	Physics	Maths
Nominated for the top 10% and gaining below a C	14%	16%	18%	13%
Nominated for the top 5% and gaining below a B	22%	28%	17%	15%

apparent success is slightly lower than if they had been included. We suggest that the limited entry in physics and French, particularly French, has inflated the apparent success in these two subjects because many of the pupils who according to our earlier evidence were incorrectly nominated did not take the O-level examination.

We were urged to carry out this analysis of examination results in order to give some evidence in relation to our earlier conjectures based on predicted scores at third form level. It is our view that the exam-based evidence is weaker than the earlier evidence but important in that it is in broad agreement with our earlier conclusions. A particular concern in the exam-based study was that only a limited number of pupils could be followed through to their examinations in all of the subjects, while a study based on predicted scores, carefully controlled for error of prediction, allowed us to include *all* the pupils of the year groups in our study.

Tables 4.18 and 4.19 can be compared with Tables 4.16 and 4.17. They show the overall percentages of pupils who would have been nominated as in the top ten and top five per cent on test scores and who later went on to take their O-levels and achieved grades in line with the test prediction.

Table 4.18: Overall percentage of pupils who were nominated for the top ability groups by tests and who achieved the expected O-level grade

	English	French	Physics	Maths
Nominated for the top 10% and gaining an A or B	65%	74%	68%	73%
Nominated for the top 5% and gaining an A or top B	48%	56%	59%	58%

Table 4.19: Overall percentage of pupils who were nominated for the top ability groups by tests and who achieved lower than the expected grade

	English	French	Physics	Maths
Nominated for the top 10% and gaining below a C	12%	17%	3%	10%
Nominated for the top 5% and gaining below a B	42%	35%	5%	17%

Within the limits of this evidence it would appear that we have broad support for the view that teachers and tests can be equally effective in the identification process. The evidence, we repeat, is stronger in English and mathematics than in French and physics because of the less restricted entry policy in these subjects. The results for the latter two subjects apply to the restricted number of pupils who actually entered for the examination, masking the teacher error that was detected in our more searching statistical work. For these two subjects we could view the level of teacher success as if it were third form nomination modified to some extent by accumulated knowledge of abilities through the third year, which will have influenced some pupils' choice of the subject. This would be further modified by accumulated knowledge of the pupils in their fourth and fifth years at secondary school, which would influence the exam entry policy for these pupils. Both of these factors would lead to a slightly higher level of apparent success than just third form nomination for the high ability groups would allow because they would cut out some of the low ability pupils from the study of examination results.

Finally, we can consider how tests and teachers might be used together in the absence of detailed classroom-based evidence. Many would suggest that test scores can complement teachers' views in the selection process by alerting us to pupils who would have otherwise gone unnoticed. It must be stated that there is a danger in this, because even though a teacher may have *intended* to use the test scores in this way he/she may become uncertain of his/her own perceptions of the pupils' abilities and unconsciously label the children with their test scores, in effect taking no account of his/her own perceptions.

It seemed worthwhile, however, to see how test predictions and teachers' perceptions might have been used appropriately to predict examination success from our own data.

Two uses of the test and teacher combination will be considered. Table 4.20 gives the details. First, we can consider a screening process in which pupils who succeed on a test criterion are then reassessed by their teachers. In this way only pupils who pass *both* test-based *and* teacher-based criteria are admitted to the more able group. Second, we can consider a process where children are allowed into the more able group if they are identified *either* by test *or* by teacher.

Table 4.20: Percentage effectiveness and efficiency of two identification strategies which make use of both test scores and teacher judgements (nomination for top ten per cent checked against an A or B success at O-level)

	English		French		Physics		Maths	
	Effec.	Effic.	Effec.	Effic.	Effec.	Effic.	Effec.	Effic.
Teacher *and* test	31	71	62	73	31	77	52	79
Teacher *or* test	69	57	91	68	86	63	92	67

In any identification strategy we can trade effectiveness for efficiency, so we look for the one that gives desirable effectiveness with acceptable efficiency. We would argue that the second method of allowing pupils into the more able group if they are on either the test or teacher list gives far superior effectiveness without the loss of overmuch efficiency. It is equivalent to a process whereby the teacher first makes his/her own assessments and then looks at test scores (of an appropriate kind) and adds to the original list those pupils who scored high on the tests but were not included by the teacher. It is a process whereby children are given the benefit of the doubt: indeed this doubt may then be removed when a further study of the children is made as a result of the work that they do, say during an enrichment programme.

A similar study of nomination for the top five per cent groups brought us to the same conclusion as that outlined above.

It was interesting to conjecture how teacher- and test-based assessments of pupils might be used together in the identification process. Some might consider that the picture would be complete after such a study. We suggest, however, that an alternative view would be to attempt refinements of teacher-based strategies. To re-state our position so far in general terms will help to focus our attention on the reasons for the following point of view.

When teachers attempted to identify third form pupils with highest potential for future performance the evidence was in favour of the hypothesis that, though the discrepancy was higher in some subjects than others, the teachers could be as effective as the tests. These teacher assessments, however, were based on crude judgements of overall ability/attainment such as would emerge from mark-book assessments modified by opinions based on limited day to day contact with pupils.

We suggest that test-based assessments are likely to remain fixed and the level of error maintained, while teachers can go on to refine their own judgements as weeks, months and years go by, reducing errors in their assessments and so becoming more effective in their strategies. There is optimism that this could be so even without a refined identification scheme. While there is some error at any stage, however, it would be wise to consider ways of trying to eliminate it because of the educational consequences that it would have for even a small number of pupils.

If we could find ways of eliminating teacher error at, say, third form level our confidence to move completely towards teacher-based identification strategies would be complete. We will see that a focus on the ways of improving teacher-based strategies moves us to consider the wider and important problem of how courses for the more able should be improved, how teachers should cooperate, particularly within a subject field, but also across year-groups and across subjects, so that the maximum number of clues to children's abilities can be accumulated.

We arrive then at one of the important questions in this context that will be considered next: is it possible to remove the bias from teacher-based assessments by means of the widely recommended method of checklist usage? This is the subject of the next chapter.

Chapter 5

The Effectiveness of Checklists In The Identification Process

Introduction

Chapter 2 contained a substantial amount of background discussion concerning the construction of checklists. We pointed out that there are a number of pitfalls to be avoided and that there are uncertainties in both the construction and the use of these checklists. An important point was that most attention in the relevant literature, up to the present, has been given to checklists of characteristics that children with high general rather than subject-specific ability might possess. Consequently little has been discovered about the validity or effectiveness of checklists designed for use in the classroom where children are taught in particular subjects.

From what we have said so far, readers might detect some uncertainty related to the use of checklists even though in principle it seems that they should help the teacher to make objective judgements of his/her pupils' ability. However, despite this uncertainty and because the errors in teacher-based judgement without checklist assistance are not enormous, we hope the checklists could go a long way to helping a teacher to decrease the remaining error. Of course this optimism should be tested by appropriate research, and it is to such research that the bulk of this chapter is devoted.

It will be useful at this stage to add to our earlier background discussion by reviewing the steps that *should* be adopted in compiling a checklist to be used in the identification process, because clearly this is an essential task for any teacher who intends to use checklists in the classroom. We will then go on to discuss our own results concerning the effectiveness of checklists. We will see too how our own study led us to deeper insights into the problems and possibilities of teacher-based assessments of the more able than we had originally anticipated.

The first stage in checklist development should be a review of the relevant literature. This should be followed by a re-assessment of the pupil characteristics that the literature review throws up, and should lead one to recast the characteristics into a list of aptitudes that relate to the pupils in the classroom. Finally, validation work should be carried out on both the individual items and the overall instrument. This should be followed by a repeat of any of the previous steps, depending on the refinements that were deemed to be necessary as a result of the validation exercise. The checklists that were used in our own work are given in Chapter 2 and serve as examples of what might emerge from this sequence of steps – though we should stress that only in mathematics were we able to undertake a direct study of the validity of individual items. We will now consider these steps in more detail.

A review of the relevant literature will help establish what is known about the separate components of ability appropriate to the particular subject under consideration. In the end this may turn out to be very little, and what there is may be just a set of opinions and value judgements as to what should be acceptable activities for children within the particular subject field. It is surprising how few of the subjects that children study at school can be clearly defined as a result of such a literature review. There is a marked lack of research evidence that establishes a set of specific aptitudes for most subjects, and demonstrates the dependence or independence of each aptitude on the others. It is also difficult to establish when a complete set of aptitudes for a subject has been isolated. These problems are partly associated with many subjects being poorly defined in terms of process variables. Perhaps we have concentrated on the products at the expense of the processes for too long in our teaching, though obviously there is a balance to be struck. Nevertheless there is room for a good deal of work to establish complete and valid lists of process variables for each of the subjects on our school curricula. In our own study we found that the work of

V.A. Krutetskii (1976) gave us the firm foundation for a mathematics checklist. Indeed this was the only one of the four subjects in our study with the solid research background that we desired. Of the other three subjects we found that science had been more clearly defined than the rest (particularly by the Assessment of Performance Unit and Schools Council), though we sensed that until more work has been done of an appropriate kind there is still room for conjecture even in science subjects. In English and French, at present there is a serious lack of background research of this kind so that it is difficult to begin the development of checklists in these subjects.

The next step is to turn the research-based checklist into a classroom-orientated instrument by relating empirically derived items to clear descriptions of aspects of pupils' behaviour which can be observed in the classroom. It can be a matter for discussion at this point which of the abilities on the checklist should take priority in the identification process, and important decisions will have to be made concerning the relevance of particular items to particular age groups of children. For example, the ability to work with mathematical generalizations may be a key item on a mathematical checklist for 13-year-olds but be inappropriate for pupils in an earlier age group.

It is interesting to speculate that for many subjects this second stage of development can be a stage of growth in awareness for an individual teacher who is faced, perhaps for the first time, with defining his/her own subject according to process rather than content headings. In subjects such as English this may be a definition of one set of goals which could turn out to be very different from those of another teacher. In the absence of background research from which to start this could lead to an ongoing difference of opinion.

It is unlikely that groups of teachers with limited resources will be able to carry out the third stage of checklist development. This is to carry out validity checks on the final checklist to establish that the items do indeed describe observable characteristics relative to the subject which the children will display, and whether the more able do perform at higher levels than the not so able on tasks related to these items. Even with the resources of a research project we were only able to carry out these validity checks on the mathematics checklist. A group of pupils with undoubted ability in mathematics (according to other criteria such as success in large-scale enrichment programmes or competitions with a high reputation) were tested on mathematical challenges designed to reveal strengths on each aptitude separately. Their results were compared with those of pupils of high, though not outstanding, overall mathematical ability. Differences were detected on each item, showing that these items were appropriate for the checklist in that children with high mathematical ability could be expected to attain higher levels of success on work relating to those items.

Thus we offer our own checklists as examples of what can be derived. Because of the checks on item validity we have more confidence in the mathematics checklist than in the lists for each of the other subjects. Physics comes a good second, in our view because of the background research on which the original choice of items was based.

It could of course be that our concern that detailed validation exercises should be carried out on each item is an over-reaction, because it is the effectiveness of the overall instrument that is important, rather than the effectiveness of each item. A validation exercise carried out on the overall instrument in a similar style to that on the individual items is the appropriate final step in the procedure. It is clear that the omission of any one of these steps in creating the checklist will lead to some uncertainty in its use, and, conversely, that the better the instrument we develop the more likely it is to assist us in making valid judgements of each pupil's ability.

Having described these steps in some detail, we will describe our own findings, based on checklist usage. We are confident that these findings are relevant to the sorts of checklists that teachers themselves might compile. Only the mathematics checklist went through all the developmental stages, but we suggest that the others represent what can be assembled from careful literature review and discussion with experts. The results should be considered with this in mind. It is worth mentioning here that our study led not only to conclusions about the effectiveness of these particular checklists, but also encouraged us to consider aspects of pupil/teacher interaction that might lead to successful use of any appropriate checklists, and to reflect on the deeper relationships between identification strategies and appropriate provision strategies for the more able.

The effectiveness of checklist-based identification

During the first year of our work teachers in our study were asked to make a second identification of their more able pupils roughly one term after they made their first (unaided) identification. In half the schools this second identification was made with the support of checklists, and in the other half without them. Teachers who used checklists were asked to complete them over a period of two to three weeks and then to use the checklist information, together with any other information which they had on the pupils, to help them to nominate pupils for the more able group. We then compared the control schools' effectiveness (without checklists) with the experimental schools' effectiveness (with checklist support) in order to establish the overall impact of checklists in the identification process. We could also check the overall difference in teacher/test agreement between the two rounds of identification to isolate any change in effectiveness that could be attributed to the fact that the teachers had taught the same children for a longer period of time.

Level of agreement between test prediction and teacher judgement

The method by which we compared teacher-based and test-based identification was the same as for the first round – i.e. teacher-based nominations for the top ability groups (top ten and five per cent) were compared with the lists of pupils ranked by their predicted O-level scores. Only minor modifications were made necessary by the small number of pupils who had left a school during the intervening months.

We have already stressed that because of the errors in the tests themselves these simple measures of *agreement* between test and teacher prediction led to tentative conclusions only about the *accuracy* of teacher judgement. However, it is worth recalling that the accuracy judgements we made in the later work on the Round 1 data were in line with inferences that could have been made from our study of agreement between test and teacher. The same proved to be true of the Round 2 data.

We will first consider the change of agreement between teachers and tests from Round 1 to Round 2. In Table 5.1, results from all the

Table 5.1: Percentage of test identified pupils also identified by teachers

	English	French	Physics	Maths
Round 2	61	54	45	61
Round 1	61	51	45	61

schools were combined. The table gives the percentages of those children identified by the tests who were also identified by the teachers.

A fascinating aspect of this table is the lack of any real improvement between Round 1 and Round 2. It was of course possible that these overall figures masked an improvement for some schools and a worsening of the situation in others. Such a variation would have been particularly interesting if it occurred between the experimental and control schools, for conclusions could then be drawn about the effect that checklists had on the second round of identification. To investigate this possibility we studied the match between teacher-based and test-based identification in the experimental and control schools separately. The results are shown in Table 5.2, together with Round 1 data from the same groups of schools, which are given for comparison.

Table 5.2: Differences between test and teacher agreement in the experimental and control schools

	ROUND 1 DATA		ROUND 2 DATA	
	% of test identified pupils also identified by teachers		% of test identified pupils also identified by teachers	
Subject	Control	Experimental	Control	Experimental
English	63	59	63	60
French	55	47	55	53
Physics	44	44	47	44
Maths	64	56	66	55

There seemed to be no evidence here that the agreement between test-based and teacher-based identification was any greater, in Round 2, in those schools which had used checklists. This was verified by significance tests based on the chi-squared test which yielded no significant difference between numbers of test-identified pupils who were selected by teachers and the numbers missed in the two groups of schools. The percentage figures quoted for Round 2 in Table 5.2 can be compared with the similar figures for Round 1. This enables us to get a first idea of the scale of the change between Rounds 1 and 2. It is tantalizing that agreement in the experimental schools in English and French was *slightly* better in Round 2 than in Round 1, whereas in the control schools the match was unchanged between Round 2 and Round 1. It may be that there is some very slight advantage in the use of checklists in English and French but we must emphasize that there is no firm evidence that this slight advantage is anything more than the result of chance.

On the basis of this measure of teacher/test agreement we were forced to conclude:

(i)   that knowing pupils for an additional term brought about no substantial improvement in the match between test and teacher judgement;

(ii)   that checklists did not lead to extensive differences between control and experimental schools in terms of this agreement.

We also explored the Round 2 data to look for differences between individual schools, between 11+ entry and 13+ entry schools and between schools of different size. No significant differences were found. This analysis took no account of test error and served as a study of *agreement* between our particular test predictions for O-level and teachers' judgements. By allowing for test error we would be able to make judgements of *accuracy* of teacher judgements in the same manner as for the first round of identification by teachers. This procedure was described in Chapter 4.

Analysis of test/teacher agreement taking some account of test error

This work is based on a repeat of the analysis discussed in the last chapter. Table 5.3 shows the percentage of Round 2 teacher nominations falling into the test-defined categories of 'good candidate for the ten per cent group', 'satisfactory candidate for the ten per cent group' and 'unlikely candidate for the ten per cent group'. Round 1 figures are included in brackets for comparison.

Table 5.3: Percentage of teacher nominations falling in the three groups 'Good', 'Satisfactory' and 'Unlikely'

| Subject | ROUND 2 DATA Percentage of teacher nominations who were: | | |
	Good	Satisfactory	Unlikely
English	61 (61)	25 (27)	14 (12)
French	54 (51)	15 (13)	31 (36)
Physics	45 (45)	24 (25)	31 (30)
Maths	61 (61)	25 (23)	14 (16)

It was interesting to discover that there was no noticeable swing of teacher judgements away from the 'unlikely' candidates in Round 2. The only subject showing the sorts of changes which might have been expected was French and even here the differences were small.

Having discovered this overall picture our next issue was to establish whether control and experimental schools differed in the way that teacher nominations were distributed across the categories. This would add to our evidence in respect of checklist effectiveness. We discovered, quite simply, that no significant differences could be detected when chi-squared tests were used to compare these distributions.

This straightforward analysis was supported by our more searching statistical procedures and the same conclusions continued to be established: namely, that *checklists, used over a short period in the way that is widely recommended, had done nothing to add to what teachers could achieve without them.*

It is interesting to reflect on the level of change that did take place on the teachers' lists between the two rounds, when some pupils who were nominated for the first round were replaced by others in the second. As we study these figures we must bear in mind that the change removed some pupils and replaced them with pupils of similar potential. The overall percentage change is shown in the following table.

Table 5.4:   Overall percentage change of pupils on ten per cent lists between Round 1 and Round 2 (control and experimental school totals combined)

English	French	Physics	Maths
16%	18%	42%	25%

In physics, the high percentage change (42 per cent) is a cause for concern. We have presented evidence that indicates inaccuracies of judgement in both rounds of identification. The high level of change in the teachers' lists produced as many 'good' candidates as before and also as many 'weak' ones. A considerable uncertainty on the part of physics teachers must be assumed.

These percentages are notably high in all subjects, so that we can be confident that in general teachers did change their opinions of some children between the two rounds of identification. Only in French was there some sign that there was a *small* increase in the overall quality of pupils selected. The overall effect between the two rounds, however, was to maintain sufficient inaccuracies in the lists of pupils in all four subjects to cause concern.

In maths and English, we have already discussed that within the terms of the test prediction Rounds 1 and 2 were equally successful. Certainly there were 'unlikely' pupils on teachers' lists, but the numbers were too small for us to conclude that the teachers had definitely made errors. *Test* error allows us to predict that there will be a number of low test scorers who eventually score high at O-level, and in the case of English and maths, this estimated number was similar to the number which actually appeared on the teachers' lists. However, the fact that a number of low scorers were replaced by a different set of low scorers overall between the rounds does suggest some uncertainty on the part of the teachers, and some error in either one round or the other.

The fact that there was uncertainty is clear; the possibility of error in one or other round rests on the following argument. If the low-scoring choices were correct in one round (and test error would suggest that they may well be), but they were replaced by other low-scoring pupils in the other round, then some of the low-scoring pupils who were nominated in one or other round must be errors - otherwise we would have to accept as correct a larger number of low-scoring nominations than the test results would suggest is reasonable. This reasoning is also valid for the other subjects, in particular for physics, where the number of changes in the 'Unlikely' category was much higher.

Finally we repeat the important conclusion: whatever changes were effected from Round 1 to Round 2 in this aspect of the work, there was no evidence to support the view that checklists made any impact on the process. This bleak though important picture was associated with checklists when teachers were asked to complete them over a period of two to three weeks. To gain some insights into why the checklists were so unhelpful we interviewed a sample of the teachers who used them. It turned out that the teachers tended to fill in the lists at one sitting.

We also strongly suspected that they tended to make overall judgements of their pupils before they filled the lists in and that these overall judgements then influenced the way in which they scored the pupils on the individual items. If the pupil had given an overall good impression, based on the sort of evidence that was at the root of the previous unaided identifications, then that pupil would tend to be given high marks on each of the checklist items if there was an absence of more appropriate information. The important point was that records of checklist clues were far too incomplete to assist in the process. The mere *possession* of even a comprehensive, well-validated checklist did not increase the teacher's ability to observe the clues to ability that the pupils might display. Indeed the clues *might not have been there* to be observed.

We followed up this somewhat disappointing result in two ways in the second year of our study. First we asked teachers of English, French and physics in some schools to use substantially the same checklists as in Year One, but to complete them over a period of a term or more, rather than in a short period of two to three weeks.

The second type of follow-up was a much more detailed study of checklist usage in mathematics.

In English the extended use of the checklist did not lead to any increase in its effectiveness. The distribution of teachers' nominations across the three test-based categories ('good candidates for the top ten per cent group'; 'satisfactory candidates for this group' and 'unlikely candidates for this group') was not significantly different in Year Two from the distribution achieved by English teachers without checklist support in Year One ($\chi^2 = 3.48$, df = 2, ns. Goodness of Fit test).

Most teachers felt that previous knowledge of the individual pupils was applied onto the lists, rather than that the lists elicited new information about the pupils. They also felt that the checklist would have been more useful had it been generated by the teachers themselves on the basis of the details of the work that they were undertaking with their pupils.

In French a similar picture emerged. Again there was no significant difference between the distribution across the three test-based categories of teachers' nominations in Year Two and the distribution of their unaided nominations in Year One. ($\chi^2 = 1.41$, df = 2, ns. Goodness of Fit test). Discussion with French teachers revealed that some checklist items were regarded as unlikely to reveal fresh information on pupils (items criticized in this way were items that dealt with familiar concepts and expressed them in familiar terminology), whereas other items which were meant to direct teachers to new insights were dismissed simply because they did deal with unfamiliar concepts in unfamiliar terms. There was again a tendency for teachers to favour a procedure in which they designed the checklist themselves with guidance from other experts rather than one in which they were asked to use a checklist imposed on them from outside.

In physics, teachers were generally supportive of the checklist items and of the modified procedure which required them to accumulate insights into pupils' abilities on these items over a period of more than a term. Certainly this general feeling of confidence in the procedure was reflected in the overall impact of checklist usage. In physics, the distribution of teachers' nominations in Year Two *was* significantly different from the distribution of unaided nominations in Year One ($\chi^2 = 6.54$, df = 2, p = 0.05. Goodness of Fit). Significantly more pupils were chosen from the 'good' category when teachers used the checklist in Year Two. This shows that the physics checklist *can* lead to an improvement in teacher-based identification. However, we would not wish to underestimate the effort that is required from the teacher if this procedure is to be used. Neither would we wish to undervalue the message that appeared from the study of English and French: namely that even if this effort is expanded, improved identification cannot be guaranteed.

We will now describe the more detailed study in mathematics. Our view is that what we have learned about the mathematics classroom has implications for other subjects as well, but, of course, we can only rely on conjecture as to the extent that this might be so.

Classroom observation and workbook scrutiny in mathematics

In order to gain first-hand knowledge of the problems and possibilities for checklist usage, we made arrangements with a sample of teachers to observe their normal mathematics lessons, so that we might record clues that children gave to their ability as these clues emerged. In this way we hoped to assess the adequacy of the clues for the purpose of building up a mathematical profile of each child. We expected that an observer might record more clues than the teacher, who would be engaged in every aspect of classroom activity. After a suitable time, we would compare results with the teacher and gain some insights into how he or she had noticed the sorts of clues that could be observed; we would also make an assessment of the adequacy of the clues for the purpose of identifying the ablest children in the class.

For the first part of the work the observer sat inconspicuously in the classroom and adopted a passive role, recording clues associated with the items on the checklist that emerged from pupil/teacher interaction, and then, at times in the lesson when the teacher responded to children's needs (such as sorting out difficulties) the observer did the same, so that only clues that would occur in the normal way would be recorded.

When there was a clear pattern of how clues to ability tended to emerge from a particular class, and after a period of time when the possibilities of valid identifications based on those clues were clear, the situation was reviewed and if necessary steps were taken to increase knowledge of individual pupils' strengths and weaknesses, to make it possible to identify the more able. We did this in ways that a teacher might adopt, either by increasing the level of challenge to the class as a whole, or by direct questioning of individual pupils within the classroom, in such a way that their responses would indicate their strengths and weaknesses.

We will illustrate the pattern of our overall findings by looking at the results for a typical class, and will show how pupil profiles emerged from both the 'passive' and 'active' phases. We assessed all the work that pupils did in their workbooks over the period of observation, but rather than marking them in the normal way, we scrutinized the books for clues associated with the mathematical profile we were trying to build up for each pupil. Finally, clues were reclassified, to build up profiles based on Krutetskii's categories, before identification of the top ten and five per cent was attempted. For this final identification, the teacher and the observer made separate judgements and then compared results before coming to their final decisions.

The teachers adopted individual teaching styles, and pupil grouping systems varied from school to school, but we would argue that the kinds of classes and styles of teaching that we observed represent what we would find in many schools and this is illustrated by our single example.

Chapter 2 contains the checklist (pages 36–8) which can be used to interpret the codes in this chapter and also an interpretation of the classroom checklist in terms of Krutetskii's list of independent aptitudes for mathematics.

The observer took on the 'passive role' for approximately half a term, sitting towards the back of the classroom with a seating plan and record sheet at hand, so that every clue to ability discerned was recorded with the pupil's name. Clues were classified as positive or negative according to whether the child showed a particular strength or weakness, and were graded as high, medium or low. In this way it was possible to categorize relative to class norms; for example it could be established where one pupil succeeded and another failed on similar work.

The teacher kept records of his/her own, as well as he/she could. The style of teaching commonly adopted was that the lessons were in two parts, the first being class teaching when opportunities arose for pupils to show abilities in response to questions from the teacher or from their own questioning, and the second part in which the pupils worked on their own, attempting to solve mathematical problems based on the class discussion. During the second activity, pupils would put up their hands to ask questions, usually when they were in difficulty. The teacher would give help as it was required. The observer continued the 'passive' role and supplemented what the teacher could do by answering some of these questions from individuals, recording any clues that were revealed. In this way it was possible to record clues as they *naturally* occurred in the lessons.

Table 5.5 shows the levels that were confidently recorded by the observer during the first phase and Table 5.6 shows the records accumulated by the teacher over the same period (half a term). These tables can be compared with each other, and it is immediately apparent that an observer with only one task in mind can record much more from the clues that come available than the teacher who is pre-occupied with all the other aspects of class activity.

Furthermore, the grading of observations that was possible for the observer was not possible for the teacher. The coding for tables based on the observer's records is ** = Grade H (high), * = Grade M (medium), − = Grade L (low). The single code for tables based on teachers records is: * = 'showed strength on this category'.

It is important to note that of the sample of classes observed this particular class produced the highest rate of clues. The teacher had a teaching style that involved a large proportion of the class in questions and answers as a topic was developed.

The profiles gradually emerged for a number of pupils and it could be conjectured that given more time Table 5.5 would be closer to completion. There were some checklist items that were not observable at all during this phase and there were a considerable number of pupils on whom decisions could not be reached for a large number of items.

Table 5.5 provided a sound basis for the second phase of activity. This is where the observer played a more 'active' role. At appropriate times, when the pupils were working independently, the observer would spend a few minutes with pupils on whom certain categories of information had not been recorded. He would chat to them about the work and pose questions that they had to tackle on the spot, related to the levels of attainment on the current work. In this way further clues could be recorded. The observer was merely

Table 5.5:   Checklist levels recorded *by observer* during 'passive' phase of observation

CHECKLIST CODES

Pupil Codes	1	2	3	4	5	6a	6b	6c	7a	7b	8	9	10	11a	11b	12	13	14	15	16	17	18	19	20	21	22a	22b
08101	*			*	**		**													**		**					
08102						*					**											**					
08103				–	*	*			*		*						*	–		–							
08104				**			**			*	*							*		*					–		
08105						*					*										*						
08106	*			*							*																*
08107																					*	*					
08108	**			**	*	*	**		*	*	**		*			*	*	*		*	*	*				**	
08109					*	*					*									*							
08110				*																							*
08111				*	*	*			*		–			*				*	*							*	–
08112					*						*							–		–						*	
08113	*			*					*	*			*														
08114					*						*									*							
08115					*						*		*					*				*					
08116				–					*									–		*	*				–		
08117	–			–					–									–		–	–	–					
08118					*				*	**															–		
08119				*	*						**							*		*							
08120	*			**	*		*			**	**	*	*	*				*	**	*	**	**	**				
08121				*		*	*				*							*				**					
08122	*			*	*		*											*									
08123	*			*	*				*	–																	
08124	*				*	*	*				*							*									
08125	*			*	*	*	*				*																
	40	0	0	56	40	60	44	0	16	32	64	4	12	16	0	4	8	28	12	44	20	40	12	0	20	4	8

Percentage of pupils who showed adequate information

Code:
** = Grade H (high)
* = Grade M (medium)
– = Grade L (low)

Table 5.6: Checklist levels recorded *by teacher* during 'passive' phase (approximately half a term's lessons)

CHECKLIST CODES

Pupil Codes	1	2	3	4	5	6a	6b	6c	7a	7b	8	9	10	11a	11b	12	13	14	15	16	17	18	19	20	21	22a	22b
08101	*			*					*	*	*											*					
08102																											
08103	*	*																*	*								
08104	*			*					*	*	*								*					*			
08105																											
08106																											
08107																											
08108		*				*	*		*	*								*	*					*			
08109																											
08110																											
08111				*										*	*												
08112				*																				*			
08113	*			*																							
08114																											
08115																											
08116																											
08117																											
08118																											
08119																								*			
08120				*						*				*	*	*								*			
08121	*	*		*					*	*	*		*								*			*			
08122																											
08123	*	*							*	*	*		*														
08124	*	*							*	*																	
08125																											
	28	20	0	28	0	4	4	0	24	24	20	0	12	8	8	0	0	8	12	4	0	4	0	24	0	0	0

Percentage of pupils who showed adequate information

Code:
* = showed strength on this category

simulating what a teacher could do during a lesson. This active questioning by the teacher, and the resulting clues about *strengths*, must be compared with the answering of pupils' questions when they get into difficulty – a process resulting in clues about *weaknesses*.

It was to some extent possible for the teacher to pursue this course of action at the same time, but for the purposes of our investigation the observer did most of the work.

As a result of the 'active' phase, Table 5.5 was updated to Table 5.7. Extra clues that the teacher recorded during this time appear in Table 5.8. At this stage there were many more gaps in the teacher's own records than in the observer's.

Table 5.7 evolved into an instrument from which confident identification could be made. Thus this teacher had a style which allowed adequate clues to be gathered from the classroom activity alone, even though he himself could not keep adequate records.

There were still some checklist items that could not be recorded, however. Items 2 and 3 (the ability to handle problems with redundant or insufficient information), item 6c (ability to solve problems of an unusual nature), item 12 (the ability to look for alternative methods) and item 22 (the cast of mind), were all very scantily observed. This implies that, even in the 'active' phase, the types of challenges set for the pupils did not allow conclusions to be reached on these items. In particular, the lack of challenge coded as 6c is of concern when one considers the requirement for high level challenges for children of high ability.

Table 5.9 records the checklist levels that were discovered from scrutiny of workbooks. The very narrow range of possibilities is quite apparent. Much of the work that pupils present in their workbooks is of a routine nature, either solving problems of a kind that the teacher has demonstrated in class (item 6a) or problems on the same topic with just minor refinements of technique (item 6b). Not all the pupils progressed to the 'hardest' questions, which could usually be categorized as 6b H; they could get by on the drill questions. When harder questions were attempted, it was not easy to associate the relevant checklist items with the pupils' work. First, it would take a good deal of time to put the clues together for each child, and second, when the pupil is not present to discuss the work, it is difficult to deduce the route that led to what was finally written in the workbook. How long did he spend on it? Did he have help? Did he try different approaches?

Table 5.7:   Checklist levels recorded *by observer* after 'active' phase of observation

CHECKLIST CODES

Pupil Codes	1	2	3	4	5	6a	6b	6c	7a	7b	8	9	10	11a	11b	12	13	14	15	16	17	18	19	20	21	22a	22b
08101	*			*	**		**		*	*	**	*	*	*				*		**		**					
08102	*			*	*	*			*		*		*	_				*		*		**					
08103	*		_	*	*	_			*		*						*	_		_							
08104	*			**			**			*	*							*		*						_	
08105	*			*		*			*		*		*	*			*		*	*		*					
08106	*			*	*				*	_	*		*	*			*		*								*
08107	*			*	*				*	_			_					*'			*	*					
08108	**			**	**	**	**	*	*	*	**		*			*	**		*	*	**		**		*		
08109	*			*		*	**		*	*	*	*						*		*			*				
08110	*				*	**			*										*		*			*			
08111	*			*	*	*	*		*		*		*	*			*	*	*						*	_	
08112	_			*	*	*	*				*			*				_	_		_			*			
08113	*			*	*				*	*			*						_								
08114	*			*	*	*			*	*	**		*		*	*		*		*			*				
08115	*				*	*	*		*	*			*					*		*		**					
08116	*			_	*	*	_		*	*	_	_	*	*		_	_	_	_	*	*			_	_	
08117	_			_	_		_			_	_	_					_			_	*	_		_			
08118	_			_	_	*				_	**						_	_	_					_	_		
08119	*			*	*		*				**	*	*		*			*	*	*					*		
08120	*	*	*	**	**		*		**	**	**	*	*				*	**	*	**	**	**	*				
08121	*			**		*	**				**		*			**	**	*	*	*	**		*				
08122	*			*	*	*					_		_					_	**								
08123	*			*	*		*		*	_	_						*	_	*						*		
08124	*			*	**	**					**		*	*			**	*	*				*				
08125	*			*	*	*	*			*	_		_			_	_	_						_	_		
	100	4	4	88	84	60	72	4	40	64	88	28	64	44	20	12	32	68	56	80	76	44	24	32	24	8	8

Percentage of pupils who showed adequate information

Code:
** = Grade H (high)
* = Grade M (medium)
– = Grade L (low)

Table 5.8: Additional clues recorded by teacher during 'active' phase

CHECKLIST CODES

Pupil Codes	1	2	3	4	5	6a	6b	6c	7a	7b	8	9	10	11a	11b	12	13	14	15	16	17	18	19	20	21	22a	22b
08101							*		*												*						
08103	*															*					*						
08104				*	*		*							*						*							
08108	*			*			*							*							*						
08112							*				*	*															
08113	*			*	*	*																					

Code:
* = showed strength on this category

It is important to consider, however, that most of the conclusions that teachers draw are based on records of attainment in workbooks. In this particular class we can tell from Tables 5.6 and 5.8 that it was not possible to draw valid conclusions from the teacher's own records of clues to ability recorded in the classroom. In contrast, the clues that the observer was able to record from the classroom were both more readily interpreted and more adequate than records from workbooks.

Table 5.10 shows the recategorization into items based on the original source (the work of V.A. Krutetskii). We recall that various checklist items referred to similar Krutetskii categories. We should note that a broad spectrum of items was observable from pupils in this class, who were from the 13–14-year age group. Nevertheless some of the Krutetskii category levels could only be determined from a limited range of checklist items. For example, Krutetskii's Category 1, 'Gathering of Information', could only be determined from clues related to one of the three possible items on the checklist (1, 2, 3) to which it was related. We can conjecture that it was the kind of mathematical provision which dictated this limitation, so that though relative abilities in this group of children showed up – the identification of the top ten and five per cent is given in Table 5.10 – the differences would be more marked if higher levels of challenge had been present.

Finally, it should be emphasized that a careful validity exercise was carried out after the decisions had been made about the relative abilities of the pupils. A large sample of pupils from all the classes involved in the study were given further mathematical challenges in an extensive one-to-one examination. The decisions that emerged from this careful follow-up study supported the decisions that were made from the classroom-based study in every case.

The close study of a sample of classrooms has enabled a number of very important points to emerge regarding the use of checklists in mathematics classrooms, which surely have echoes in classrooms where other subjects are taught. We have found particular points from different kinds of teaching environment, but our most telling conclusions are of a general nature. We recall that the original sample of schools were representative of the County of Oxfordshire and that in general terms the effectiveness of checklists from the first part of our work was very small throughout all of the schools in the sample. The fact that we have isolated some general points from the second part of our work from a sample of these schools leads us to suggest that these discoveries are applicable to many more schools of the kinds from which our sample was drawn.

We will, now, bring together the main findings of this study, as follows:

(a) The rate at which clues to pupils' ability occur in the classroom depends on the teaching style adopted. One extreme is the style which allows for a large amount of class cooperation and discussion to develop a topic. This tends to absorb a large amount of class time on whole group work. The other extreme is where there is very little whole class activity and this time is spent quite formally, with minimal pupil participation, introducing a topic. The majority of the time is spent on individual work from text-book or worksheet.

The former method encourages a wide variety of clues to ability to emerge, but the teacher finds difficulty in recording these clues, being preoccupied with the development of the lesson. For certain pupils who fully cooperate the challenges can be at a high level.

The latter method encourages only a narrow range of clues to emerge, and challenges are at a low level. This method, however, allows more time for a teacher to respond to individual pupil's needs during the time available for quiet work. Clues to ability can emerge from this interaction. If, however, a teacher responds only to the pupils in difficulty, weaknesses rather than strengths are observed.

Table 5.9: Checklist levels recorded from workbook scrutiny, accumulated over 'active' and 'passive' phase

CHECKLIST CODES

Pupil Codes	1	2	3	4	5	6a	6b	6c	7a	7b	8	9	10	11a	11b	12	13	14	15	16	17	18	19	20	21	22a	22b
08101	*					**	**			*										*		*					
08102	*					**	**			*										*							
08103	*					**	*			*																	
08104	*					**	*			*										*		*					
08105	*					**	*																				
08106	*					**	*			*										*		*					
08107	*					**	*			–										–							
08108	*					**	**													*		*					
08109	*					**	*			*				*						*							
08110	*					**	*			*										*							
08111	*					**	*			*										*							
08112	*					**	*			*										*							
08113	*					**	*			*										–							
08114	*					**	*			*										*					*		
08115	*					**	*			*										*		*					
08116	*					**	*			*																	
08117	*					**	–			*										*							
08118	*					**																					
08119	*					**	**			*										*							
08120	**					**	**							*						*		*					
08121	**					**	**			*										*		*					
08122	*					**	*			*										*							
08123	*					**	*			*										*							
08124	*					**	**			*										*		*					
08125	*					**	*																				
	100					100	96			80				8						30		32			4		

Percentage of pupils who showed adequate information

Code:
** = Grade H (high)
* = Grade M (medium)
– = Grade L (low)

Table 5.10: Recategorization of information from Table 5.5 to Table 5.8 for the purposes of identification of top ten per cent and top five per cent

Pupil Code	1A (1,2,3)	2A (4,5,6,21)	2B (7,8)	2C (9,10)	2D (11,12,13,19)	2E (14,19,20)	2F (16)	3A (17,18)	4 (22)	Identification level
08101	*	**	**	*	*	*	**	**		top 5%
08102	*	**	*	*	*	*	*	**		10%
08103	*	–	*		*	–	–	*		
08104	*	**	*			*	*			
08105	*	*	*	*	*	*	*	*		10%
08106	*	*	*	*	*	*			anal/log	10%
08107	*	*	–	–		*	–	*		
08108	**	**	**	*	**	*	**	**		5%
08109	*	**	*	*		*	*			10%
08110	*	**	*			*	*			
08111	*	*	*	*	*	*	*		spat geom	10%
08112	–	*	*	*			–	–		
08113	*	*	*		*	–				
08114	*	*	**	*	*	*	*			10%
08115	*	*	*		*	*	*	**		10%
08116	*	–	*	–	–	–	–	*		
08117	–	–	*	–	–	–	–			
08118	–	–	*			–	–			
08119	*	**	**	*	*	*	*		spat geom	10%
08120	**	**	**	*		**	*	**		5%
08121	**	**	**	*	**	**	*	**		5%
08122	*	*	–	–	*	–	*			
08123	*	*	–		*	–	*			
08124	*	**	**	*	*	**	*	*		10%
08125	*	*	–	–	–	–				

Code:
** = Grade H (high)
 * = Grade M (medium)
 – = Grade L (low)

It should be noted, of course, that these conclusions apply to classrooms in which worksheets and text-books are not prepared with the more able specifically in mind. If such preparation is done there can be little doubt that clues to abilities can be extracted more directly as pupils are engaged on the work discussion and observation as well as from assessment of the completed work.

(b) In every class studied it was possible to achieve a full profile judgement on all pupils. In none of the classes were the teachers able to record clues to ability adequate for reliable identifications to be based on them, neither was the observer able to gather enough information from passive observations, though in all cases he was able to record much more about the pupils' abilities than was the teacher. In each class observed, the recording of additional clues became the responsibility of the observer, though the means of increasing pupil response was a cooperative exercise between teacher and observer. Evidence from one school, however, demonstrated that it was possible for the teacher herself to keep such records and to increase the availability of the full range of clues to ability.

(c) There were two methods of increasing knowledge of pupils' abilities. First the teacher could scan the records kept and see where knowledge of particular pupils was lacking, and then during an appropriate part of the lesson could engage that pupil in mathematical activity that would reveal knowledge of a particular aptitude. Confirmation of what appeared as strengths or weaknesses could be gradually sought over further lessons until a confident profile emerged. Second, if there were certain checklist items that were not filled in for a large proportion of pupils, the teacher could assess if the pupils were being adequately challenged and exercised on this particular aptitude. Lessons could be deliberately modified to bring in such challenges. These two approaches were crucial to both adequate provision and identification. It did not prove possible in any school to identify pupils properly without engaging in the former activity *in a most deliberate way*. The need for the latter activity must be of major concern if able pupils are to be fully nurtured in the subject, and in every class that was observed much of the work was predominantly routine and produced a very limited challenge.

(d) Workbook scrutiny produced a very limited range of confident clues. Again, this must be compared with the wealth of knowledge to be gained by discussing work with the pupil rather than trying to make judgements just from workbooks. The manner of assessment that was used to classify knowledge of pupils' ability gained from the workbooks was of course different from the normal grading and recording a teacher will carry out. However, the implication is that assessments of whatever kind based on workbook knowledge must be based on this narrow range of clues. If we add to these workbook clues the minimal number of clues that teachers were able to record from within the classroom in the normal run of lessons, we begin to understand how, when presented with decisions on who ranks as most able, the limited knowledge could be misleading and biases of numerous kinds begin to have their affect on the kinds of pupils rated as highly able.

(e) An observer's ability to record clues to ability better than a teacher whose attention is on many other matters is an important point which could be exploited. A strategy for identification could well be to invite an observer into the classroom for a sufficient number of lessons to plot profiles of pupils' abilities for the purposes of identification. A small number of lessons may suffice to show the teacher where further pupil/teacher interaction is needed in order that he or she might complete the profiles alone. This teamwork could lead not only to better identification but also to a review of the adequacy of provision.

(f) Certain checklist items were underchallenged and hence hardly observed, even when positive steps were taken to improve the variety of clues to ability. Here, again, we have conclusions which emerge from the relationship between identification and provision.

Pupils were rarely given problems of the 6c variety, that is, problems that were of a nature requiring exploitation of a wide range of knowledge or mathematical insight. More is required than just a challenge from a set of miscellaneous exercises, though very little time was generally given for even this. We are thinking of problems for which there is no obvious prescription. Too often the work, even for the most able, was repetition of routine questions (6a) or slight deviations (6b). Within these '6c' problems we would expect deeper challenge of many of the checklist items: handling of large amounts of information, from which the relevant information has to be isolated and often where there is inadequate information (items 2 and 3); the production of logical proofs, (items 4, 5, 6); the exercise of the aptitude for flexibility in devising and understanding proofs, (items 12, 13); the seeking of a variety of solutions from which an elegant one emerges (items 14, 15).

One particular item that was, at best, tentatively recorded was 'mathematical cast of mind'. It may be that at third-year level clues could not be strong enough to detect particular bents (spatial or analytic). Inevitably, therefore, the clues that were picked up emanated from a wide range of mathematical topics. It was possible to judge pupils in relative terms as a consequence of the level of work presented, mainly by extending the challenge within these '6a and 6b' types of problems with individual pupils. Perhaps the most appropriate suggestion is that when pupils have displayed their profile of strengths in the identification process, in relation to the normal classroom challenges, the sorts of challenges that these pupils are given should be reassessed so that they might exercise these strengths and be allowed to escape from the constant and limiting repetition of routine work. This may not be seen as the most appropriate course for others in the same class who have weaknesses on the profile, though a gradual strengthening of these weaknesses may be considered necessary.

(g) It was shown that it is *possible* to make valid identifications of pupils entirely a result of checklist usage. It is interesting that our previous work was concerned with an identification to be measured against test prediction for O-level performance. In the later checklist work, and because of the validity of the checklist, we escaped from the O-level criterion and made valid judgements of *present* mathematical aptitude, rather than potential for the future.

The consequence of this is that we can be confident in our ability to monitor pupils' development based on what we are at present observing in them, and to modify our judgements of needs and abilities from week to week. Our provision can be appropriate to the broad spectrum and we are freed from the arguments associated with any narrowness of identification from tests or for an examination such as O-level. Indeed we can have the broad rather than the narrow challenges of examinations such as O-level fully in mind for the appropriate pupils because of a full knowledge of them and the spectrum of abilities.

(h) The effort required for proper identification must not be underestimated. We discovered that positive steps were needed to work with individual pupils and this should be done over a considerable number of lessons; we cannot expect to set ourselves a few lessons to complete the task. The most appropriate interpretation of this is that it should affect the teaching style once and for all. We could even be so bold as to suggest that the effort put into this classroom activity – where the pupil's workbook will also be under some scrutiny as a basis of the interaction – could be offset by the need for routine marking of the traditional kind. With limited time available for all of the activities that a teacher considers appropriate, less class workbook scrutiny would enable lessons to be prepared in an appropriate fashion to meet the variety of individual needs of pupils across the mathematical spectrum.

(i) Identification was concerned with the top ten and five per cent, relative to the school norms, but the accumulated knowledge of individual pupils made it clear when a pupil of high calibre relative to national norms had been discovered. As it turned out, we had no difficulty in separating the top percentiles from the rest 'by eye', so to speak, rather than by statistical analysis. This must be encouraging for a teacher who lacks the resources for statistically orientated work.

It is with optimism then that we close this chapter; optimism that if a teacher is able to fulfil what we consider is an obligation to take steps to know his/her pupils as individuals, then identification of able pupils based on classroom interaction can be completely valid. If, however, the appropriate steps are not taken, the degree of error reported earlier in this and the last chapter is likely to remain. In the next chapter we will review the sorts of biases that can exist in these identification strategies.

CHAPTER 6

Factors Which May Influence Teacher Judgement

Introduction

At this point it is useful to repeat that our study revealed only a small degree of error in identifying more able pupils on the part of English and mathematics teachers. Indeed, in any one round of identification, the mismatches between these teachers' nominations and those based on pupils' test results could be accounted for entirely by the magnitude of the error in the *test*.

In physics and French the mismatches between teacher-based and test-based nominations were greater, and large enough to imply that teachers themselves had made some mistakes. Nevertheless, once test error had been accounted for, some 70 per cent of teacher-based nominations in each of these two subjects were entirely satisfactory pupils. The overall picture of teacher-based identification in the subject-specific context is therefore a rather more optimistic one than can be inferred by reference to earlier research on high-IQ pupils.

However, there was *some* error in the nominations made by teachers and we therefore feel that it may be helpful to present one further strand of evidence relating to teacher-based identification. This concerns the pupil characteristics which distinguish teacher-selected pupils from other pupils. This evidence therefore sheds light on the biases that teachers might need to overcome if they are to refine their identification strategies. In some ways it would have been appropriate to place this chapter before the discussion of checklists and how they might be used effectively, but we did not want the reader to end on a note of undue optimism which might override the proper concerns which should be associated with teacher-based identification programmes. There is a danger of forgetting that it is only by taking very positive steps that some misleading factors which influence a teacher's judgements can be overcome. By reminding the reader at *this* point of these influences and by going some way to demonstrating their nature, we hope the optimism will remain but that it will be a cautious optimism.

In the absence of research evidence one can only speculate on what might characterize a teacher's judgement in the identification process. Even if some surprising pupil characteristics are associated with teacher-based selection, it should certainly not be inferred that teachers made a conscious decision to select pupils with these characteristics. For example, it is very unlikely that a teacher would consciously choose all of the neat, well-behaved pupils in a class and label them as more able. It is not, therefore, a straightforward matter to discover either if biases exist or to find out what these biases might be.

It may not even be the case that it was the pupils' neatness that *unconsciously* caused the teacher to select them as more able. Neatness may have been correlated with other more appropriate characteristics to which the teacher was responding. (In some of our analysis we were able to explore this kind of possibility.) Alternatively the fact that they were recognized as 'more able' by the teacher may have been communicated to the pupils who may have responded by giving more attention to their work and, incidentally, may have become more neat. What our study of the characteristics of teacher-selected pupils can do is to alert *teachers* to the kinds of factors which *might* lead them to label a pupil as 'more able', and to alert other *researchers* to factors which might usefully be subjected to an experimental study which could itself establish the causal nature of the link.

Because of the possibility that pupil characteristics may *unconsciously* affect teachers' judgements, it may not be useful to ask teachers themselves if they suspect that certain factors influenced their judgement of pupils. The method of enquiry that we used, therefore, was to look for evidence in a number of directions. Although each piece of evidence has its own limitations, each was taken as contributing to an overall pattern which would establish, more firmly than any single piece of evidence would allow, those factors which *were* associated with teacher-based selection as teachers made their assessments of pupils.

Some preliminary clues came from a study of the level of agreement between tests and teachers. If there had been evidence of gross misjudgement then we might have expected to find a number of quite inappropriate characteristics associated with teacher judgement. On the other hand if there was evidence of only a small amount of error then we might suspect more appropriate characteristics to be strongly associated and less appropriate ones to be weakly associated with the pupils selected by the teachers. The less appropriate characteristics might then be more difficult to detect. Indeed, we might expect the nature of the pupil characteristics which influenced judgement to differ from teacher to teacher. It might also be that for each teacher there was no consistent characteristic detectable: for example, one child might be favoured because of his/her home background, another because of neatness of presentation of work. The evidence from our study of the accuracy of teacher-based identification was, indeed, optimistic so that we might expect that the biases would not be crude, but that they might be hard to detect.

Before discussing the three main and complementary sets of evidence it is worth reminding the reader of our strong suggestion that *appropriate* use of checklists can provide one method of removing whatever biases do exist. Another may also be possible, and we have discovered a little evidence that it is. It may be that, by being made aware of their particular biases, teachers may be able to train themselves away from them. Perhaps the most effective method would be a combination of a self-awareness exercise in which a teacher becomes aware of the sorts of pupil characteristics that influence his or her judgement, followed by training in the use of checklists.

Having set the scene we are now in a position to review the sets of evidence which will highlight the conclusions that gradually emerged from this part of the study. The first of these was associated with the test-based characteristics of pupils selected for the high ability groups by their teachers. The second and third concerned the descriptions that teachers made of their pupils, first in semi-structured and then in highly structured interviews.

Test-based characteristics of the pupils who were nominated as more able

The complete set of background test scales has been listed in Chapter 2. By finding those test scores which correlated most highly with teacher-based selection we were able to isolate in an objective way clues to any biases which existed. The strength of the evidence is limited by the relationship that exists between the scales and the actual influences on teacher judgement. In some situations, for example, bias towards a particular sex might be detected directly by our statistical procedures. In others we might expect that bias towards, say, high motivation of pupils might only be shown up indirectly from this study because of the difficulty of assessing motivation directly by using the tests which we used. We might, however, gain a *clue* to the bias if a number of attitude scales correlated quite highly with teacher-based selection.

It was important for us to choose the most appropriate statistical technique to isolate the best evidence. If we had used the Pearson product moment correlation coefficient directly then it would have been difficult to isolate the main correlates. This is because the test scores themselves are intercorrelated. For example, attitude C (academic self image) might be correlated with attitude B (relationship with teacher) for a particular class of pupils, and there may well have been a reason for this in that the pupils' self-confidence may have been influenced by the teacher's reactions to them. It could be that the teacher actually favoured children with whom he/she had a good relationship, but because of the association between scales B and C, both scale C and scale B would turn out to be correlated with teacher selection, even though the true bias was in favour of scale C. It was possible for us to isolate the main characteristics of teacher selection and eliminate these secondary characteristics by employing a process of partial correlation. This is a device whereby statistical controls can be applied to one variable in order to assess the independent influence of another. The variables that appear in Table 6.1, therefore, are those which remained highly correlated with teacher selection after partial correlation had allowed us to isolate them as the main characteristics when the teacher-identified group was compared with the rest of the year-group.

Table 6.2 casts this evidence into another form showing the total number of schools (out of 13) which had each variable as a strong characteristic of teacher selection.

Table 6.1: Table showing the Pearson correlation coefficient for those variables that independently distinguish between the teacher selected groups and the whole year group (Round 1)[1]

School	Subject	Significantly correlated variables
00 (157)	English	VR (0.45) NA (0.40) SR (0.34) LU (0.48)
	French	VN (0.63)
	Physics	C (0.41) VN (0.52) SR (0.49)
	Maths	NA (0.59) SR (0.38)
01 (218)	English	VN (0.54) LU (0.53) ORIG (0.32)
	French	VN (0.58) NA (0.53)
	Physics	NA (0.40) VN (0.40) MR (0.36)
	Maths	VN (0.53)
02 (192)	English	SP (0.47) LU (0.53)
	French	LU (0.44) SP (0.43) VN (0.44) C (0.30) D (0.34)
	Physics	VN (0.47) C (0.29) E (0.23)
	Maths	NA (0.56) C (0.33)
03 (162)	English	FLEX (0.40) VN (0.39) SP (0.39) B (0.28)
	French	LU (0.44) NA (0.45) CSA (0.37)
	Physics	VN (0.49) MR (0.39)
	Maths	NA (0.52) B (0.33)
04 (196)	English	LU (0.54) SP (0.51) B (0.37)
	French	LU (0.39) A (0.32) B (0.32)
	Physics	SR (0.28) A (0.27) LU (0.33)
	Maths	NA (0.54) C (0.33)
05 (166)	English	VN (0.42) C (0.33) SP (0.43)
	French	VN (0.50) SP (0.43) LU (0.48)
	Physics	VN (0.49) FLEX (0.30) C (0.30) MR (0.44)
	Maths	NA (0.64) C (0.39)
06 (202)	English	LU (0.54) B (0.44) C (0.41) FLEX (0.38) NA (0.40)
	French	LU (0.53) B (0.37)
	Physics	VN (0.52) B (0.44)
	Maths	NA (0.52) C (0.42)

07	English	VN (0.48) C (0.38) SP (0.41) LU (0.43)
(284)	French	VN (0.39) LU (0.40) SP (0.39) A (0.26) C (0.35)
	Physics	VN (0.45) SR (0.45)
	Maths	VN (0.57) C (0.43) SR (0.44)

08	English	VN (0.45) SP (0.49)
(130)	French	LU (0.34) VN (0.36)
	Physics	VN (0.35) FLEX (0.33) ORIG (0.32) B (0.27)
	Maths	NA (0.54)

09	English	VN (0.55) LU (0.58) ORIG (0.30)
(240)	French	ORIG (0.32) VR (0.54) SP (0.50) LU (0.57)
	Physics	VN (0.56) LU (0.53) MR (0.43) C (0.27)
	Maths	VN (0.54) LU (0.51)

10	English	VN (0.57) LU (0.60)
(128)	French	LU (0.55)
	Physics	VN (0.48) B (0.30) C (0.40)
	Maths	VN (0.50)

11	English	VN (0.52) B (0.27)
(127)	French	VN (0.56)
	Physics	VN (0.41) SR (0.42)
	Maths	VN (0.32) NA (0.52) VR (0.42) SR (0.43)

12	English	LU (0.46) SP (0.42) NA (0.35)
(129)	French	SP (0.37)
	Physics	VN (0.52)
	Maths	VN (0.56)

[1] The significance of correlation in all cases is at the 0.1% (***) level. Pearson correlations are in brackets next to the variable name. The number of pupils is in brackets under the school code.

It is not surprising that the strong characteristics of the group varied from subject to subject (this matched our overall subject-specific viewpoint which was brought out by the regression equations, in that abilities required for success in a subject were different for each subject). It is surprising that the characteristics differed so much from school to school and that they were not always the expected indicators of ability (for example, we found NA

Table 6.2: No. of schools showing each test as an independent characteristic of its 'top ten per cent' group after partial correlation

Variable	English	French	Physics	Maths
Creativity				
FLU	0	0	0	0
FLEX	2	0	2	0
ORIG	2	1	1	0
Attitudes				
A	0	2	1	0
B	4	2	3	1
C	3	2	6	5
D	0	1	0	0
E	0	0	1	0
F	0	0	0	0
G	0	0	0	0
I	0	0	0	0
DAT				
VR	1	1	0	1
NA	2	2	1	8
VN	9	7	12	6
AR	0	0	0	0
CSA	0	1	0	0
MR	0	0	4	0
SR	1	0	4	3
SP	7	4	0	0
LU	9	9	2	0
Neatness (NT)	0	2	0	0
Social Class (SC)	1	2	0	2

Note:
Sex, being a categorical variable, is not really suited to this analysis and is omitted from this table, and from Table 6.1.

(Numerical Ability) to be a characteristic for French in School 01, LU (Language Usage) for maths in school 09). On the basis of the regression equations used for predicting an O-level score for each pupil, one would hope to find that in every school the table would show LU as a strong characteristic in English and French, MR (Mechanical Reasoning) and NA in physics, NA and possibly SR (Space Relations) in maths. However, we actually found that good attitudes were strong characteristics in some schools, and some subjects. This was particularly so for attitude B (relationship with teacher) and attitude C (academic self image). Neatness, creativity and social class were also independent characteristics in a small number of schools (though they were by no means consistent independent correlates of teacher selection). (This was discovered by chi-squared analysis which was a more suitable analysis for this variable.)

The general academic ability scale VN (VR plus NA) was a characteristic of teacher-selected pupils in most subjects and in all schools. In physics, in particular, this characteristic was an independent correlate of teacher-based selection in 12 of the 13 schools. One might suppose that, though it is not a wholly inappropriate correlate of selection in physics, it may be too closely associated with the teachers' view of what counts as high ability in that subject. The absence of MR (Mechanical Reasoning) in physics in all but four schools would indicate a bias towards the less valid general ability measure VN and away from the more valid one (MR). This may well be due to lack of real knowledge of pupils at third-year level because of the limited teacher/pupil contact which is so often a characteristic of physics teaching in the early years of secondary schooling. The bias towards general ability may also be a result of the fact that work in science up to third-form level may not be sufficiently challenging to pupils' specific scientific aptitudes, so that teachers do not get very much information about their pupils' strengths and weaknesses in these areas. An interesting implication is that to improve teacher-based identification, we might need to look to syllabus content and to teaching style as well as to the process of selection itself.

High scores on attitudes, on one or other of the scales, were characteristics of teacher-selected pupils in nearly half of the identifications, high scores on attitudes B (relationship with teacher) and C (academic self image) occurring most frequently. High creativity as measured by fluency, flexibility or originality did not characterize many of the teacher-selected groups.

Importantly, social class and neatness were not usually characteristics of teacher-selected pupils, once the effect of the correlations between these and other variables had been accounted for. Sex was a variable that could not reasonably be analysed in this way but its independent influence can be assumed to be no stronger than was determined from the uncontrolled Pearson correlation coefficient. Only in French did a noticeable number (5) of the teachers in individual schools show, among other influences, a sex bias – and this was consistently in favour of the selection of girls. Only one school in physics and none in English or maths demonstrated a significant association between teacher selection and sex difference. Since this part of the work gives fairly strong indications of the variables which did not have a dominant influence on teachers, we are led to conclude that the influences of social class, neatness and sex (variables which are often thought to be powerful in influencing teachers' judgements) were weaker than is commonly supposed: and, in fact, these crude biases were far less noticeable than other in some ways more encouraging biases, in the sense that a 'fine tune' of the identification process might lead to their elimination.

Of the variables included in these tables, no differences that relate to types of school were apparent. For example, the 13+ entry schools (02, 05, 09) did not show markedly different characteristics from the rest of the sample. The overriding view was that differences were more often differences from teacher to teacher than from one school type to another.

To add to this data we were able, via a questionnaire to pupils, to obtain some information on their likes and dislikes, on whether they thought a subject was useful or not, and on whether they thought they were good at a subject. These factors could have influences on their performance in a subject, and could affect the teachers' judgement of their ability. For each subject, we counted how many chosen, and how many not-chosen pupils gave a positive response, by including the subject in their answers to requests such as:

'List the subjects which you think you like'
'List the subjects that you think will be important to you when you leave school.'
'List the subjects that you think you are good at.'

The analysis by school and subject is summarized in Table 6.3 where we quote the number of schools (out of 13) that showed significant difference between the teacher-selected group and the rest of the third year on each question.

Table 6.3: Number of schools showing significant difference on questions relating to subject popularity, when the teacher-selected group is compared with the rest of the year group

	Like/dislike	Useful/not useful	Think good at
English	3	0	6
French	12	9	13
Physics	8	7	8
Maths	7	0	10

Where differences occurred they were always in the expected direction for the questions: that is, the teacher-selected group tended to like the subject, thought the subject useful and thought that they were good at the subject.

There is strong evidence that French selection was biased towards those who liked French and those who thought they were good at it in almost all schools. Pupils' opinions of their own abilities in maths also seemed to be generally important.

The noughts in the 'Useful/not useful' column for English and maths perhaps reflected a tendency of both identified and not identified groups to think the subjects useful.

There were no detectable differences between school types from the analysis of pupil attitudes outlined above.

One wonders how much this difference in pupils' views of their own abilities actually affected their performance in the subject. It is also interesting to note that there were large numbers of those who were not identified who thought themselves good at the subject. This could of course be because their assessments were made relative to the expectations within their own particular class.

In conclusion, it would appear that there is no *great* cause for concern about the characteristics of the teacher-selected group compared with the whole school, in the sense that the biases were in directions which could be removed, it is reasonable to suppose, by training or self awareness. There is, however, *some* concern that emphasis was not always strong on the most relevant characteristics. If judgement of ability was adequately sensitive to the special characteristics of high potential in each subject area, one would hope that general ability would be given less weight. Individual teachers did seem to have individual biases and there was no one type of school environment in which they were particularly successful in identifying more able pupils. Perhaps the most powerful conclusion was that social class, neatness and sex did not appear to have an overwhelming influence on teachers' judgements in the individual schools. The nature of the findings from this part of the study was in line with our expectations when we considered that the level of teacher success in the identification process was relatively high.

Informal interviews with teachers

The second source of evidence comes from the interviews held with teachers. In a way this evidence came indirectly. When we found that there were a relatively small number of pupils whose ability was a source of dispute between teachers and tests we thought that the teachers might have observed certain characteristics in these children that the tests did not detect, so we asked them to describe these pupils in order that we might note the characteristics down.

At the outset we might have expected the teachers to give wide descriptions of each child. For example, we might have heard about a choice for the mathematics list: 'Very good at geometry, vivid imagination, captain of chess club, plays piano at grade 6, always keen to appear in school play, enjoys the challenge of puzzles, scientific background at home . . .' Instead of this we received rather limited pupil descriptions.

In French, physics and mathematics, in all schools (including those schools where checklists had been used in our preliminary work and where we might have expected much more subject-specific description of pupils to be given) we were given just brief descriptions containing a limited number of separate ideas about each pupil. The comments consisted mainly of generalities concerning both ability in the subject and attitudes and behaviour.

The brevity of the information is emphasized by the large number of individual aptitudes on which comments *could* have been made. For example, these could cover the range of characteristics which appear on the subject-specific checklists that were reported in chapter 2. The same could be said of English though here there were rather more comments related to specific aspects of performance.

There were two possible reasons for the superficial nature of the responses. First, it may have been difficult for the teachers, in an interview situation, to verbalize all that they knew and felt about the pupils. Second, their knowledge of them may have been limited.

We believed that each of these was true to some extent but the important point was that there was almost certainly a lack of the detailed subject-specific knowledge we had hoped for. If this had not been so we would have had, within the descriptions of the pupils, much more detail. Rather than such generalities as 'good exam performance', we would have got a series of descriptions such as 'Spatially aware', 'Good mental arithmetic', 'Never gives up with a problem', and many more such as these.

Some examples of the pupil descriptions are given in the following table. There may be strong echoes in these descriptions of the sort of comments that so often appear alongside marks of attainment on end of term reports to be taken home by pupils.

Table 6.4: Descriptions of pupils by their teachers

English

Pupil 1	Does well without hard work. Natural ability but lazy. Interest in literature. Likes what is easy. Accurate on technical skills.
Pupil 2	Quite hardworking. Bright and humorous. Useful boy to have in classroom.
Pupil 3	Careless at first. Now trying hard. Tremendous reader. Highly independent. Trying to overcome punctuation problems. Spelling not too bad.
Pupil 4	Uncommunicative. Lacks concentration. Mechanically accurate. Writes immaculately.
Pupil 5	Immature.

Pupil 6   Keen. Not outstandingly bright. Articulate. Normal for age.

Pupil 7   Bright. Superficial interest in English.

French

Pupil 1   No real prospect in French. Chronically inaccurate. Orally weak.

Pupil 2   Orally fair. Written work sloppy.

Pupil 3   Has become lazy since the beginning of the year. Not committed.

Pupil 4   Enjoys French. Conscientious girl. Very accurate technically.

Pupil 5   Able. Successful in tests.

Pupil 6   Orally strong. Enjoys the subject. Potential O-level.

Pupil 7   Reliable worker. Not outstandingly clever, but very well motivated.

Physics

Pupil 1   Lazy worker. Slipping now, not committed, very casual. Father pushes. Showed interest and put in a lot of work on an open evening. Backs away from school work.

Pupil 2   Was picked as a result of exam, other information would not confirm. Not standing out in Year 4 2nd set. Doesn't ask/answer much.

Pupil 3   Not a stroke of work in year – did well in exam. Not outstanding in Year 4, not doing homework, smoking, generally getting into trouble. Brother in Oxford and suffers from comparison.

Pupil 4   Went off to end of 3rd Year. Now reckon him to be top 20 per cent, not top 10. Enthusiastic, hard working, seems to have aptitude but struggles with subject. Positive attitude.

Pupil 5   Intense concentration, very good work, enthusiastic, making good use of what he's got. Not doing quite as well now.

Pupil 6   Dramatic improvement this year, not industrious. Responds well to maths side, quiet, overshadowed by dominant brother and sister.

Pupil 7   Good trier, very quiet, better exam than classwork. Maths now bringing her down.

Mathematics

Pupil 1   Lazy. Underperforms.

Pupil 2   Quiet. Could be underperforming.

Pupil 3   Bright. Works hard. A little underconfident.

Pupil 4   Poor at English but good at maths.

Pupil 5   Asks if needs help. Not particularly hardworking.

Pupil 6   Industrious. Not so good under pressure. Needs to build confidence.

Pupil 7   Works slowly. Poor eyesight. Methodical. Has natural insight.

Pupil 8   Difficult home environment. Not always consistent, but achieves good results quite often.

It is useful to categorize the complete set of comments obtained from all these interviews under the four subject headings, as is done in the next table. Many of the comments required us to be subjective in our classifications and no reliability exercise was carried out on these data. Nevertheless, we would suggest that there would be little disagreement in the overall weight of the conclusions drawn from this part of the work and expressed in the percentages in Table 6.5.

Table 6.5: Classification of pupil descriptions from the interviews with teacher

| | PERCENTAGE OF COMMENTS THAT RELATED TO: | | |
	Specific aptitudes relating to the subject	General impressions of ability in subject	Attitude/ behaviour/ motivation	Other
English	27	36	24	13
French	16	28	42	14
Physics	10	12	48	30
Maths	3	40	51	6

From these examples and even more clearly from the whole set of interview comments we can see that teachers tended to be very brief in their descriptions of the pupils, almost to a dismissive level at times. We were left with a feeling that the pupils were judged on general ability for the subject, modified by opinions relating to their general motivational characteristics. This gives the same sort of picture that emerged from the study of test-based characteristics.

In very few cases was a specific aptitude mentioned though it should be said that teachers of English seemed more able to give specific descriptions of the pupils than other teachers. In all subjects, however, there was a lack of the detailed knowledge of pupils that we had hoped for.

The fact that general ability for a subject was quoted as opposed to a list of specific abilities may have been a result of the fact that many of the children judged as able had high ability in a large number of specific aptitudes. We doubted that the teachers could remember these specific details accurately so that the generalized comments that they made were associated in part with this. We conjecture, therefore, that their accuracy of assessment was relatively high because they noticed the majority of pupils who had displayed an overall spectrum of abilities, but that errors were possible because of the lack of detailed knowledge of borderline pupils.

The modification of judgement associated with motivational factors was the cause of some concern. Undoubtedly motivation is important (see, for example, Entwistle, 1968), in that potential may not be realized if the pupil does not turn his/her attention to the subject in a positive way. However, if teachers were judging on motivation alone some pupils of high ability would have been missed. It is interesting to note that the ratio of motivational comments to ability comments is especially high in physics.

The data collected from these interviews are revealing in their own way and lead us a little further towards an understanding of why there was a degree of detectable error in the teacher-based identification strategies. We also have amplification of the point of view expressed in the last chapter where we discussed the careful procedure that should be adopted if classroom observations are to be the basis of totally reliable identification schemes.

The next piece of work adds further amplification to these points of view and might stand as an answer to those who suggest that teachers' descriptions of pupils were incomplete not because of their lack of knowledge of the pupils but because they lacked ability to verbalize that knowledge.

Personal construct approach

This final complementary strand came from what could be viewed as a much more structured approach to interviewing the teachers. The approach was based on the personal construct methodology first described by Kelly (1955). This assumes that people assess others on a number of dimensions (or constructs). The set of constructs used by any individual may have constructs in common with the sets used by other individuals, but it is, essentially, his or her own set of *personal* constructs. As such it may contain constructs which are not commonly used by others. The first step of a personal construct study is, therefore, to elicit from individuals the particular set of constructs which they use. In our work this was done with six English teachers, four French teachers, 11 physics teachers and six mathematics teachers. A selection of constructs elicited is given in Table 6.6, which includes the results of the work with one teacher in each of the four subjects. (For compactness only one pole of each construct is shown.)

The picture that emerged from this part of the study confirms our previous ideas: teachers' knowledge of pupils was expressed in terms of rather broad generalizations concerning their abilities, and of views of the pupils' motivation and attitude. The method that we employed seemed to elicit the constructs more freely than did the informal interviews, and later work (which is not discussed here) allowed us to extend our insights in a number of directions. These led us in particular towards an understanding of which of the pupils' characteristics may have influenced the judgements of teachers.

Table 6.7 shows the percentage of constructs that emerged from our sample of teachers which could be classified under the same broad headings that we used before.

It is very interesting that for the two subjects in which teachers were less effective more constructs in the attitude/motivation/ personality column emerged, re-emphasizing our general finding that in the absence of more appropriate criteria teachers may be biased towards the kinds of characteristics that come under this heading. In English, a more accurately judged subject, a relatively

Table 6.6: Examples of constructs that emerged from the triadic elicitation exercise

Construct	Construct
English	French
Fluent writing – many ideas	Confident
Sensitive, expressive writing	Sees patterns in French clearly
Poor comprehension	Extrovert
Makes basic mistakes	Careful/fastidious
Good vocabulary	Able
Good grammar	Well motivated
Good ideas for essays	Brighter
Lively mind	Determined to make progress
	Good at applying knowledge
	Highly able in languages
	Cooperative
Physics	Mathematics
Good overall physics ability	Interested in mathematics
Absorbs day to day work	Fast worker
Enthusiastic	Strongly motivated
High self-motivation	Keen on maths
Scatterbrain in work	Accurate worker
Low accuracy in physics written work	Cooperative
	Mature
Lacks commitment to academic work	Tries hard
	Serious attitude
Poor understanding of concepts	Keen to please
Lacking in confidence	Gets very confused
Spontaneous interest in physics	Disruptive
Poor practical skills	Casual attitude
	Overconfident
	Untidy work

high proportion of observed characteristics was related to individual subject-specific aptitudes.

We saw in chapter 5 that there was evidence in the study of the mathematics classroom to suggest that teachers *could* overcome existing biases through careful use of appropriate checklists. It can be conjectured that knowledge of the kinds of biases (outlined above) that a teacher might develop could be overcome by self training. It may be, however, that an appropriate element of an

Table 6.7: Classification of constructs emerging from the triadic elicitation exercise

	PERCENTAGE OF COMMENTS THAT RELATED TO:			
	Specific aptitudes relating to the subject	General impressions of ability in subject	Attitude/ behaviour/ motivation	Other
English	38	19	38	5
French	4	26	61	9
Physics	12	17	64	7
Maths	11	29	47	13

in-service training course would be in the direction of developing awareness of possible biases, together with training in the construction and use of checklists. These two complementary exercises would seem to have great importance and potential. It may be that a short course of training is needed before a teacher can make effective progress in overcoming existing biases.

Tantalizingly, there is only a relatively small amount of teacher error in pupil assessment to be overcome, but it may be that the bias is so deeply ingrained that it requires a major commitment to remove it. We believe that the effort required for this should not be underestimated. Further, we suggest that the need to overcome the biases might be considered as a duty on the teachers' part. If a teacher cannot come to know his or her pupils in such a way that he or she can describe them fully on an aptitude profile for the subject, then how can those pupils be challenged at an appropriate level on that aptitude profile? There is still much research to be done in the area of teacher training, but we can provide a hope that it might be effective in helping to remove teacher bias. In a small-scale study we found that it was possible to direct a teacher away from the inappropriate characteristics that influenced the identification process and were detected in our personal construct work, hence moving that teacher towards a more successful identification strategy.

Having discussed our sets of complementary evidence regarding teacher bias, we have gone some way towards discovering the nature of teacher judgement error when able pupils are selected on the basis of clues gained from pupil/teacher interaction. Our overriding conclusion was that teachers did not have in-depth knowledge of a subject-specific profile for each of the pupils. The way in which they *did* know and classify pupils was broadly in line with a generalized view of pupils' abilities, however, so that the level of error we discussed in previous chapters could be expected. We can assume that in the case of some pupils generalized views of ability will be subject to modification, and that when these modifications are made, the levels of error that we reported when teachers are asked to select a high ability group can be induced. We have seen, importantly, that the modifications are often associated with views of the pupils' behaviour, personality and motivation for the subject.

This evidence, when put alongside our other evidence, helps us to paint a clear picture of the problems and possibilities associated with the identification of pupils with high ability in a particular subject. We have now reached the point where we should summarize our overall results and look at some of the major implications of our work.

Chapter 7

Summary Of Conclusions And Discussion Of Related Topics

We hope that the reader will have detected an important thread which binds together the issues taken up in the previous chapters. At the outset our investigation was concerned with one straightforward set of questions associated with teacher effectiveness in the identification process. We were concerned with the top ten per cent and smaller subgroups of third year (13-year-old) pupils in four subjects and in a representative sample of schools in one county in England. By studying these questions in depth we have brought to light a number of other interesting insights that were not originally contemplated. It is appropriate at this point to summarise our main findings, briefly reflect on the side issues and then close by giving our own view of the way the issues bind together.

Pupils of high ability in more than one subject: We have found evidence that the number of pupils who have high ability in a large number of subjects is quite small. There is agreement between test-based and teacher-based assessment on this issue. This strongly supports a subject-specific focus for identification of, and provision for, the more able and for any system of grouping applied to pupils as a whole; otherwise, pupils of high ability in one subject may be unfairly overlooked.

Test/teacher agreement: The level of agreement between teacher-based assessments of pupils with high ability and test-based measures of potential, tested in a subject-specific way, was far higher than previous research in the area of general academic ability implied. The level of mismatch between test-based and teacher-based nomination in English and mathematics was so low that there was no evidence suggesting teachers made more than a few errors in their nomination of able pupils. Nevertheless there were a number of high scoring pupils omitted from the teachers' lists, and a number of low scoring pupils were included on the lists. In French and physics there was sufficient mismatch between test-based and teacher-based nomination to indicate actual errors of judgement on the teachers' part. Too many high scoring pupils were missed from the teachers' lists and too many low scoring ones were included for the mismatch to be accounted for entirely by the error present in the test-based assessment of O-level potential. If we take these subjects as representatives of a major part of the secondary curriculum it seems that there is some cause for concern in all subjects. However, in English and maths (and by extrapolation in other subjects where teachers have more opportunity to work with individual pupils and where pupils study the subject for a reasonable length of time before identifications have to be made) this concern is much less marked.

School differences: There was no detectable difference between schools of different types (large/small, schools with their main intake at 11/those with their intake at 13) in relation to the levels of teacher/test agreement.

Bias in teachers' judgement: Evidence from a number of sources reinforced the view that there was some inaccuracy in teachers' judgements of pupils' potential. Certain pupil characteristics seemed to be associated with teacher-based selection. These varied from teacher to teacher but there did not seem to be significant differences between schools of different types. Pupils' social class and sex were not always associated with teacher-based selection though biases of this kind could be detected in some of the teachers' lists. There was an indication that physics teachers identified pupils with high general ability, rather than those with high ability on other criteria which were more relevant to physics ability. This effect was most noticeable when identifications were made early in the year, and was not so evident for identifications made later in the year when the teachers had taught the pupils for longer. Physics teachers also tended to nominate pupils with good motivation or good attitude towards their work. If physics can be taken to represent the sciences we might suppose that the conclusions would extend to other science subjects, at least at third-form level. There was strong evidence that children who had favourable attitudes to the subject were also selected by the French teachers. Again, if French can be taken as a representative of the languages, this important conclusion is more widely relevant. Teachers in general were found to modify their judgements of pupils' abilities by opinions relating to the motivation and attitudes of their pupils. It can be conjectured that this is so when the teachers lack the more specific detail appropriate to aptitudes for the subject.

Identification for provision: One implication was that, though teacher identification of those pupils who could obtain a good O-level pass in the subject (particularly in mathematics and English) may have been reasonably successful, the mapping, by teachers, of pupils' individual strengths and weaknesses *within the subject* was not very detailed (although English teachers were somewhat better than others). It is clear that without this detailed knowledge the structure of the teaching and of the challenges set to the pupils in the subject cannot take full account of these strengths and weaknesses.

Compilation of a valid subject-specific checklist: It was demonstrably clear that the compilation of a suitable subject-specific checklist is not a straightforward matter. This is because of the uncertainty that exists between teachers as a whole as to the specific aptitudes which constitute, and should be developed through, the teaching of their subject. In the case of mathematics, it was possible to compile a valid checklist because previous research in the subject had clarified the nature of these specific aptitudes. Even though we have discovered that there is considerable difficulty associated with the use of checklists, it must remain a priority for teachers to agree on the profile of aptitudes that make up their subject whether it be for purposes of guiding identification or structuring provision. A clear need for the sort of research in other subjects that provided the background to the mathematics checklist has been implied by our study.

The effectiveness of checklists in the identification process: The physics checklist was of some help in guiding teachers' judgements when it was filled in over several months. However, there was clear evidence that checklists were not usually effective instruments in guiding the identification process when teachers were asked to fill them in for each pupil, by drawing just on recent observations and memories of the pupils' abilities. There is strong evidence that teachers did not have the detailed knowledge of the pupils on the broad spectrum of subject aptitudes that would be required for this exercise unless very deliberate steps were taken to work in an appropriately challenging way with individual pupils. The lack of sufficient clues to ability that would enable a subject-specific profile to be built up for each child was confirmed by observation of the mathematics classroom. It was discovered that sufficient clues were not observable in the children, nor, of those clues available, were adequate records kept by the teacher, the latter being due to the preoccupation with other classroom activities. However, we discovered it was possible to gather sufficient clues to ability if the teacher took deliberate steps to do so. This was accomplished by the teacher spending more time with individuals than would occur naturally. Appropriate challenges could be presented to an individual from which a range of clues could emerge. It was also possible to observe more clues to ability if the work given to the class was varied, in order to challenge the pupils more broadly.

Workbooks: In mathematics, a very limited range of clues to ability could be extracted from children's workbooks, so that appropriate classroom activity was the main vehicle to valid identification. The force of this conclusion within other subject fields can only be based on conjecture, but in subjects where the nature of the work put into exercise books is restricted in its width of challenge, as was clearly demonstrated for mathematics, then the clues to ability that emerge from the marking of the pupils' work are similarly restricted.

We can now move on to a number of the general issues.

A second observer

We discovered from the work in mathematics how much more a

second teacher could record concerning the individual abilities of the pupils in a class than could the teacher at the front, who was engaged in all the activities that are involved in delivering a lesson. This was mainly because of the single-minded approach that the second observer could adopt.

We suggest that the boost to checklist profile construction that a second observer can give a class teacher is considerable. The effort required to provide an extra teacher for a sample of lessons could be compared with the effort that could be saved if it were no longer necessary to administer and mark psychological tests. We argue that the use of a second observer is potentially a very interesting basis for the identification of the more able and that it should be given careful consideration.

Identification through provision for a larger group

Often we want to identify able pupils in order to give them extra, more appropriate learning experiences. Often too, we are constrained by the numbers of pupils that we can handle in such programmes of extra provision, especially if these take the form of tutorial teaching or summer school activity and so on. If this is so we must seek a method that identifies an appropriate number of pupils accurately. However, when there is more flexibility over numbers, we could adopt the strategy of asking teachers to nominate the pupils without any test or checklist support, without the in-service training that we will discuss later, and we could agree to allow in more than the number for whom the provision was designed. This provides for any pupils about whom the teacher feels some uncertainty. The level of provision would be for the same high level of ability, so that when the pupils were taking part the teacher could begin to pick out those who could not reach the levels required to continue with the provision programme. If the way in or out of the enrichment group was easy, there would be few repercussions for the child who needed to drop out.

It may be that if teachers are asked to nominate a small number of pupils for a summer school, as an alternative to one of the procedures discussed above, they might begin by choosing a larger group for some extra provision *in school* and then make their final selection from this group in the way we suggest.

We would suggest that this method is in line with our findings and applies to whatever level the provision is aimed at. For example, when we asked teachers to nominate their top ten per cent most of the top five per cent on test marks were included, so that if our provision were for the top five per cent, allowing the top ten per cent in during the initial stages of the provision would enable us to find the right pupils.

The selection could be entirely dependent on teacher nomination, and might rely on no more than the teacher's day-to-day knowledge of the pupils.

In-service training

In our work we discovered that teachers were often uncertain about what can be expected of and what should be provided for an able child in their subject. More specifically we have found that their ability to recognize able children was influenced by pupil characteristics that often seemed to be rather inappropriate. Since these influences were, no doubt, predominantly subconscious, it is very difficult for a teacher to gain the feedback which is necessary to enable him or her to make adjustments to the things which he or she allows to influence judgement. We suggest that our work provides a basis on which teachers could be helped to refine their understanding in this area. It is interesting to speculate that the characteristics of teacher-selected children revealed by the study could be used as a starting point for a series of discussions with teachers about identification.

Pupil grouping

We can only reflect briefly on this issue, but would be wrong to neglect it completely.

There are a number of ways in which pupils can be grouped for teaching purposes. Whenever decisions are made connected with ability grouping, an identification strategy has to be employed. The effects of mistaken placement of pupils of high ability in low sets is well known. We have studied the ability of teachers to nominate children of high ability, and found that errors are made in all subjects, but much more strongly in some than in others.

Some of the errors were made before the third form teacher drew up his or her lists, so that some pupils whom tests assessed as having high ability were not even considered. The system had already condemned these pupils by placing them in low sets or streams. It would seem that if the needs of all of the more able are to be best served, children should at least begin their early secondary school career in mixed ability groups and that the transition from this type of grouping to another based upon ability should occur only when sufficient information has been assembled to enable this to be done in a subject-specific way. A wide range of tests (not just IQ tests), teachers' opinions guided by checklists, and teachers' opinions honed by the in-service training that we have suggested, may all have a part to play in building up the package of information upon which this subject-specific setting might be based.

In putting forward this view that a mixed ability start would be advantageous to able pupils it is interesting to note that the Banbury Grouping Enquiry (Postlethwaite and Denton, 1978) found that able pupils who spent their first year in mixed ability groups gained slightly better examination results than those who had spent their first year in streamed groups. Furthermore, the evidence that we have provided regarding the relatively small number of pupils who were of high ability in a large number of subjects provides a strong warning to those who favour a rigid policy of streaming across several subjects on the basis of general ability alone.

There are, therefore, organizational implications in some of our findings, as well as implications for individual teachers who wish to improve their own ability to select able children from the classes that they teach. If we do not take up both of the issues in a positive way we may fall well short of our duty to the able children in our care.

Checklists as an aid to provision

The subject-specific approach to identification that we investigated led us to study the independent components of ability that are related to each subject. The checklist so formed was used for the purpose of aiding identification, but another view suggests that the checklist actually defines a subject in its broadest sense. If so the checklist should be the headings under which we devise appropriate forms of provision for the more able. We would argue that this leads to a carefully structured scheme of enrichment. This approach as well as being recommended for general application has been used in a further phase of work which aims to evaluate classroom-based provision for the more able. This topic, it is hoped, will be the subject of a further book of this series.

Summary

We suggest that those who seek to make judgements of the abilities of pupils should be encouraged to develop strategies that rely more on the day-to-day clues to ability that pupils display, as a result of the challenges set to them, than on test measures of performance.

We are encouraged to recommend this because, even when teachers' judgements were made on the basis of rather superficial knowledge, our evidence supported an optimistic view that the judgements could be as effective as those which relied on a carefully developed test predictors for O-level. Furthermore, we have shown that a teacher-based identification scheme could be developed to a degree where considerable confidence could be placed on the outcome of the identifications.

On the other hand, the extra effort required of a teacher who seeks to eliminate bias of judgement should not be underestimated. First, the teacher must understand the conceptual structure of the subject in detail. Second, he or she must introduce challenges to the pupils that will reveal appropriate clues to ability, and then be able to recognize abilities as they are displayed, and relate them to the aptitude profile for the subject. We would recommend that teachers adopt a style of teaching that allows them to work more with individuals and small groups than with a class as a whole.

Though we have no evidence that in-service teacher training leads to any greater success in the identification process, we suggest that the kind of expertise that many teachers would need to acquire in order to implement a bias-free identification strategy could most readily be acquired from a short course of training.

It was quite evident from our work that the extent to which a teacher could get to know his or her pupils was constrained by other classroom tasks. It was also clear how much more easily an observer could gather appropriate information from which the identifications could be made. We suggest, then, that the strategy of using a second observer in the classroom should be carefully considered. It could be argued that time spent on this activity would be time saved if it was no longer necessary to administer a series of standardized tests. It could also be argued that the involvement of more than one teacher in the lessons of a class would bring the additional rewards associated with team teaching, where preparation of the challenges given to the children and the overall strategy of class management could be the result of team effort.

An important consequence of teacher-based identification is that in planning ways to observe clues to ability, a teacher becomes aware of the kinds of challenges that he or she is giving to the pupils, so that in addition to the benefits associated with identification, areas that required educational enrichment would be revealed.

The need to keep accurate records of the abilities that pupils display has been clearly demonstrated. In the absence of these records a teacher's memory of specific abilities seems to fade, so that judgements based on memory alone are likely to be based on overall impressions. We have shown that these impressions can be influenced, in particular, by judgements about the attitudes of pupils. These records should be of the checklist format which builds up a subject-specific profile of abilities rather than the usual mark-book summaries of attainment. We would warn teachers away from decisions concerning pupils' abilities which are based on conventional marking of workbooks alone, partly because of the very limited range of abilities that may have led to the mark-book assessments, and partly because of the difficulty of recalling which marks related to the occasional pieces of work that had been of a searching nature. We would suggest that discussion with pupils as they work is likely to lead to a much more comprehensive picture of the pupil's abilities than a scrutiny of just the workbook, in isolation, would produce.

When time is limited we suggest that priority be given to preparing lessons which contain appropriately high and individualized challenges, though we warn that this could be at the expense of time spent on routine marking. Again, there are benefits to be gained from this strategy, both for the level of provision that would result and for the opportunities that could be created concerning knowledge of the full range of pupil abilities.

In cases where full records have not been compiled but where records of a general nature have been kept, and where it is necessary to identify a certain number of high ability pupils for a purpose such as admission to an enrichment programme of summer school, we suggest carrying out a teacher-based identification of a larger group of pupils than the desired number. The smaller group might be identified by observation of and discussion with the pupils as they tackled work of a challenging nature, as the preliminary stage of a provision programme.

The method of record keeping we have recommended should be used continuously, and records be brought up to date at frequent intervals. They should also be accumulated from year to year. It is important to take account of the fact that some abilities, such as the ability to make mathematical or scientific generalizations, which may not be apparent in one year group (say 11-year-olds) may develop later (say at age 13), and this developmental rate may differ from child to child. Opinions about pupils' abilities should then be modified as the abilities develop. In this respect it is important that pupils have the opportunity to be challenged to an appropriate and individual level at each stage of their development. This points us towards a mixed ability style of teaching in all groups even if the groups were formed on a system of separation into ability sets.

As a final telling comment, we started this book with an air of concern about what might be viewed by some as a small elite. We developed the notion that the group we were talking about might well be quite wide, however, but even more interesting is the point that if we scan through the major conclusions that are put forward from the study, for the main part we could offer those same conclusions for the education of *all children*.

Appendix 1

Further details on the construction of the prediction equations

Table A1: Examination courses on which the predictive equations are based

	English	French	Maths	Physics
School 13	01	0120	052	Nuffield
School 07	01	020	052	Nuffield

Separate predictors were established for the 1977 and 1978 entries. The 1978 cohort at the two schools were tested for differential aptitude (DAT) in their third year, while the 1977 cohort were tested in their fourth year. In order to have a common level on which to measure, the DAT scores for the 1978 entry were adjusted to take account of this. This we accomplished most easily by using percentile markings. A pupil's score on a particular scale was checked for its percentile rank based on the NFER national norms for fourth-year pupils and he was then given the corresponding score for that percentile from the third year national norm table. No adjustment was necessary for attitudes or creativity because pupils in both years did the tests at the same time in their school career, but a small adjustment was necessary in the examination scores obtained in the two year-groups. This adjustment was made within each grade in each subject. The range of scores for a particular grade in 1978 was compared with the range for a particular grade in 1977 and the 1977 mark was adjusted by the appropriate amount. Since this adjustment was of the order of three or four marks in 150, for the majority of cases a simple ratio adjustment within each grade was thought to be adequate.

For each subject, the prediction equation was derived by Multiple Regression Analysis. Very briefly the procedure was that a matrix was established showing the correlations of each test score with every other test score, and the correlation of each test score with O-level result. The matrix was inspected to discover which test scale correlated most highly with O-level performance – and, therefore, which test scale was the most effective predictor. This scale became the first scale in the prediction equation. Inspection of the matrix continued to identify other scales which could be combined with the first to improve the prediction ability of the equation, and these scales, if found, were then included with appropriate weights. The procedure, which was automatically carried out by computer, did not rely on any subjective judgement of which test scale *should* be a good predictor for O-level, but simply indicated which combination of scales was *in effect* the best predictor.

It is worth pointing out that the combination of tests that were associated with each prediction equation gave us better measures of potential than any one test alone, including a test of general ability. The predictive ability of IQ tests has received some attention in the literature, giving further support to this point of view. Both from the theoretical and the empirical standpoint, there is evidence to suggest that IQ is *not* the most appropriate measurement for the assessment of subject-specific potential. As discussed in Chapter Two, Guilford's model of the intellect and similar multidimensional models of intelligence provided some theoretical basis for such a view. Empirical support for the view that general ability, as measured by IQ, is not a particularly good predictor of subject-specific ability, can also be found in the literature. For example, Vernon has quoted correlations between IQ and School Certificate subject results which range from .51 (mathematics) and .50 (English), through .38 (history) and .39 (chemistry) to .12 (biology) and −.02 (art). Thus, even in the cases of mathematics and English, only some 26 per cent of the variance in School Certificate results was explained by IQ. A similar picture has also been obtained by the present Project. We have shown that the percentage variance in 0–level scores explained by IQ was 15 per cent (English), 14 per cent (French), 22 per cent (physics) and 24 per cent (maths). Fuller details are given in Table A2 below.

Table A2:   Relationship between O-level score and the General Ability Scale VN

Subject	Correlation	No. of pupils	% Variance explained
English	.39	171	15
French	.37	79	14
Physics	.47	109	22
Maths	.49	151	24

It was this evidence and discussion with psychologists at NFER that suggested to us that these levels of prediction could be improved upon by using the group of tests outlined above. Roughly a hundred pupils who were in their 3rd year in 1974 and 1975 had gone on to take O-level examinations in each of the subjects. It was therefore possible to establish, by means of Multiple Regression Analysis, relationships between pupils' test scores at 13 and their subsequent performance in each of the chosen subjects. The resulting prediction equations, when applied to the data from subsequent groups of 13-year-olds in this present study, were used to generate pupils' predicted O-level scores. It is these predicted O-level scores which we have interpreted as objective measures of potential. For immediate comparison with Table A2 we summarize in Table A3 the correlations and percentage of explained variance that resulted from the prediction equations.

Table A3:   Relationship between O-level score and predicted O-level score calculated from the prediction equation

Subject	Correlation	No. of pupils	% Variance explained
English	.60	146	36
French	.70	68	49
Physics	.66	92	44
Maths	.57	130	33

Extensive use was made of the SPSS (Nie, Hull, Jenkins and Steinbrenner, 1975) programme for Multiple Regression Analysis to seek the best predictors for the four subjects. Early attempts were concerned with both O-level and CSE prediction on a combined scale, but the most confident approach was concerned with prediction for O-level alone because of the problem of combining two sets of examination results into a single scale. Prediction for an Examination Grade was seen as rather coarse so we investigated the possibility of deriving a predictor for actual scores at O-level.

We were fortunate to gain the cooperation of the Oxford Delegacy of Local Examinations who released O-level scores for the two year groups of the two schools for mathematics, French and English. The Oxford and Cambridge Board also kindly cooperated to release the Nuffield Physics results. All of this was approved by the schools themselves. This enabled us to satisfy more closely the requirement of regression analysis that the scales should be interval, and we now had much more information than could be contained in the pupils' grade alone.

The numbers of pupils involved in the analysis were as follows:

Table A4

1977 exam

	Total No. in year group	Nos. entered for O-level			
		Eng	*Fr*	*Phys*	*Maths*
School 13	429	82	74	51	70
School 07	160	43	24	22	40

1978 exam

	Total No. in year group	Nos. entered for O-level			
		Eng	*Fr*	*Phys*	*Maths*
School 13	365	61	40	63	62
School 07	180	55	17	16	25

We were thus concerned with a predictor for examination success within the group of candidates who were entered for O-level. Since the whole spectrum of results were included we were confident that this predictor could be applied to the whole group in our study of the more able. A second caution was concerned with the particular examination for which our equations predict. The two schools followed the same examination syllabus in all subjects except French, so that we were able to pool results on all but French. Because of the small numbers taking French in one school, the prediction equation for French was derived for the sample of pupils from the school with the largest entry. Though the prediction equations were related to particular syllabuses we were confident in our approach of using them to predict the potential of pupils for the top ten per cent in other schools because many schools use these syllabuses and also because the particular syllabuses we have used have much in common with others, especially as they affect work at third form level.

Bibliography

ASSESSMENT OF PERFORMANCE UNIT (APU) (1978). *Science Progress Report, 1977–78*. London: HMSO.
ASSESSMENT OF PERFORMANCE UNIT (APU) (1978). *Language Performance*. London: HMSO.

BARBE, W.B. and RENZULLI, J.S. (1975) *Psychology and Education of the Gifted*. New York: Irvington.
BARNES, D. (1980). 'Situated speech strategies. Aspects of the monitoring of oracy, *Educational Review*, **32**, 2.
BENDER, M.P. (1974). 'Provided versus elicited constructs', *British Journal of Social and Clinical Psychology*, **13**.
BENNETT, G.K., SEASHORE, H.G. and WESMAN, A.G. (1974). *5th Manual for the Differential Aptitude Tests*. New York: Psychological Corporation.
BRIDGES, S.A. (1964). Gifted Children and the Brentwood Experiment. London: Pitman.
BRIDGES, S.A. (1975). *Gifted Children and the Millfield Experiment*. London: Pitman.

CHRONBACH, L.E. and MEEHL, P.E. (1955). 'Construct validity in psychological tests', *Psychological Bulletin*, **52**.
CITY OF BIRMINGHAM EDUCATION COMMITTEE (1979). *Gifted and Outstanding Children*. Birmingham.
CLARKE, G. (1981). Guidelines for the recognition of More Able Pupils. (Draft.) London: Schools Council.
CLARKE, G. and CUTLAND, P. (1977). *Identifying for Provision*. Middlesborough: Cleveland County Council.
COOK, M. (1979). *Perceiving Others*. London: Methuen.
CUNNINGHAM, C. *et al.* (1978). 'Use of SOI abilities for prediction', *The Gifted Child Quarterly*, **22**, 4.

DEVON COUNTY COUNCIL (1977). *Find the Gifted Child*. Exeter: Devon Education Dept.
DENTON, F.C.J. and POSTLETHWAITE, K.C. (1982). The Identification of More Able Pupils in the Comprehensive School. (Unpublished final report to the DES.)

EARNSHAW, H.G. (1974). *Criterion and Assessment in English.* Aldershot: Associated Examining Board.

EASTERBY-SMITH, M. (1981). 'The design, analysis and interpretation of repertory grids'. In: SHAW, M.L.G. (Ed) *Recent advances in Personal Construct Technology.* London: Academic Press.

EGGLESTON, J.F., GALTON, M.L. and JONES, M.E. (1976). *Processes and Products of Science Teaching.* London: Macmillan.

ELASHOFF, J.D. and SNOW, R.E. (Eds). (1971). *Pygmalion Reconsidered.* Worthington, Ohio: Charles A. Jones.

ENTWISTLE, N. (1968). 'Academic motivation and school attainment', *Brit. J. of Educ. Psychol.*, **38**, 2.

EYSENCK, H.J. (1967). 'Intelligence assessment', *British Journal of Educational Psychology*, **37**.

FREEMAN, J. (1979). *Gifted Children Their Identification and Development in a Social Context.* Lancaster: MTP Press.

FREEMAN, J. (1981). 'Some emotional aspects of giftedness'. In: GRUBB, D.W.H. (Ed) *The Gifted Child at School.* Oxford Society for Applied Studies in Education.

GETZELS, J.W. and JACKSON, P.W. (1958). 'The meaning of giftedness', *Phi Delta Kappan*, **40**, 2.

GETZELS, J.W. and JACKSON, P.W. (1962). *Creativity and Intelligence.* New York: Wiley.

GUILFORD, J.P. (1959). 'Three facets of the intellect', *American Psychologist*, **14**, 8, August 1959. Reprinted in: BARBE, W.B. and RENZULLI, J.S. *Psychology and Education of the Gifted.* New York: Irvington.

GUILFORD, J.P. (1967). *The Nature of Human Intelligence.* New York: McGraw Hill.

HALL, E. (1978). *Using Personal Constructs*, Rediguide series. Nottingham: Univ. of Nottingham, School of Education.

HER MAJESTY'S INSPECTORATE (1964). *The Eighth Report of the Secondary Schools Examination Council on the Examining of English Language.* London: HMSO.

HER MAJESTY'S INSPECTORATE (1977). *Gifted Children in Middle and Comprehensive Secondary Schools.* London: HMSO.

HER MAJESTY'S INSPECTORATE (1979). *Aspects of Secondary Education.* London: HMSO.

HOLBROOK, D. (1961). *English for Maturity.* Cambridge: Cambridge University Press.

HOLLINGWORTH, L.S. (1942). *Children Above 180 IQ.* New York: Yonkers-on-Hudson.

HOYLE, E. and WILKS, J. (1980). *Gifted Children and their Education.* London: HMSO.

JENKINS, E. and WHITFIELD, R.C. (1974). *Readings in Science Education*. London: McGraw Hill.

KELLY, G. (1955). *The Psychology of Personal Constructs*. New York: Norton.

KERRY, T. (1980). *Teaching Bright Children, Teacher Education Project*. Nottingham School of Education (mimeographed).

KERRY, T. (1981). *Teaching Bright Pupils in Mixed Ability Classes*. London: Macmillan.

KRUTETSKII, V.A. (1976). *The Psychology of Mathematical Abilities in Schoolchildren*. Chicago: University of Chicago Press.

LONDON ASSOCIATION FOR THE TEACHING OF ENGLISH (LATE) (1965). *Assessing Compositions*. London: London Association for the Teaching of English.

LAYCOCK, S.R. (1957). *Gifted Children: A Handbook for the Classroom Teacher*. Toronto: Copp-Clark.

LEVINSON, B.M. (1956). 'Rethinking the selection of the intellectually gifted'. *Psychological Reports*, **2**.

LOMBROSO, C. (1891). *The Man of Genius*. London: Scott.

LOVELL, K. and SHIELDS, J.B. (1967). 'Some aspects of the study of the gifted', *British Journal of Educational Psychology*, **37**.

MARLAND, S.P. Jr. (1972). *Education of the Gifted and Talented*. Report to Congress by the U.S. Commissioner for Education, Vol. 1. Washington D.C.: US Office of Education.

MARTINSON, R.A. (1975). *The Identification of the Gifted and Talented*. Virginia: Council for Exceptional Children.

MASSEY, A.J. (1978). 'The relationship between 0- and A-level Nuffield physics results', *Educational Research*, **20**, 2.

MEEHL, P.E. (1954). *Clinical Versus Statistical Prediction*. Minneapolis: University of Minnesota Press.

MURPHY, R.J.L. (1981). 'O-level grades and teachers' estimates as predictors of the A-level results of UCCA applicants', *British Journal of Educational Psychology*, **51**.

NFER Publishing Company (1982). *Catalogue of Tests for Educational Guidance and Assessment*.

NIE, H. *et al.* (1975). *Statistical Package for the Social Sciences*. New York: McGraw Hill.

NISBET, J.F. (1895). *The Insanity of Genius*. London: Deloa Nore Press.

OGILVIE, E. (1973). *Gifted Children in Primary Schools*. London: Macmillan.

OGILVIE, E. (1980). 'The Schools Council curriculum enrichment project'. In: POVEY, R. (Ed) *The Gifted Child*. London: Harper and Row.

OSKARRSON (1975). *The Relationship Between Foreign Language Proficiency and various Psychological Variables*, Stuttgart, 4th International Congress of Applied Linguistics.

PARKYN, G.W. (1948). *Children of High Intelligence: a New Zealand Study*. Oxford: Oxford University Press for the New Zealand Council for Educational Research.
PEGNATO, C.W. and BIRCH, J.W. (1959). 'Locating gifted children in high schools: a comparison of methods', *Exceptional Children*, 25, 7.
PIMSLEUR, P. (1964). 'Underachievement in foreign language learning, *International Review of Applied Linguistics*, 2.
POSTLETHWAITE, K.C. and DENTON, F.C. (1978). *Streams for the Future?* Banbury: Pubansco.
POSTLETHWAITE, K.C. (1984). Teacher-based identification of pupils with high potential in physics and English, unpublished D. Phil. Thesis, Oxford.
POVEY, R. (Ed) (1980). *Educating the Gifted Child*. London: Harper and Row.

RENZULLI, J.S. and HARTMAN, R.K. (1971a). 'Scale for behavioural characteristics of superior students', *Exceptional Children*, November 1971.
RENZULLI, J.S., HARTMAN, R.K. and CALLAHAN, C.M. (1971b). 'Teacher identification of superior students', *Exceptional Children*, November 1971.
RENZULLI, J. and SMITH, L.H. (1977). 'Two approaches to the identification of gifted students', *Exceptional Children*, 43.
RENZULLI, J.S., REIS, S.M. and SMITH, L.H. (1981). The Revolving Door Model, *Phi Delta Kappan*, May 1981.

SCHOFIELD, B., MURPHY, P., JOHNSON, S. and BLACK, P. (1981). *Science in Schools Age 13: Report No. 1.* (A.P.U.). London: HMSO.
SHIELDS, J.B. (1973). *The Gifted Child*. Slough: NFER Publishing Company.
SIEGEL, S. (1956). *Non Parametric Statistics*. New York: McGraw Hill.
SOLOMON, R. (1979). 'Identifying gifted children', *Journal of Applied Educational Studies*, 8, 2.
STEVENS, F. (1970). *English and Examinations*. London: Hutchinson Educational.
STRAKER, A. (1981). *Mathematics for Able Pupils*. London: Schools Council.
SUTTON, C.R. and HAYSON, J.T. (1974). *The Art of the Science Teacher*. London: McGraw Hill.

TEMPEST, N.R. (1974). *Teaching Clever Children 7–11*. London: Routledge and Kegan Paul.

TERMAN, L.M. *et al. Genetic Studies of Genius.* (Vol.1: TERMAN, 1925. Vol.2: COX, 1926. Vol.3: BURKS, JENSEN and TERMAN, 1930. Vol.4: TERMAN and ODEN, 1947. Vol.5: TERMAN and ODEN, 1959.) Stanford: Stanford University Press.

THURSTONE, T.G. (1941). 'Primary mental abilities of children', *Educational and Psychological Measures,* **1**, 12.

TILSLEY, P. (1979). 'Gifted children and their education', *Journal of Applied Educational Studies,* **8**, 1.

TORRANCE, E.P. (1961). 'Problems of highly creative children', *Gifted Child Quarterly,* 5.

TORRANCE, E.P. (1965). *Gifted Child in the Classroom.* New York: Macmillan.

VERNON, P.E. (1957). *Secondary School Selection.* London: Methuen.

VERNON, P.E. (1961). *The Structure of Human Abilities.* London: Methuen.

VERNON, P.E., ADAMSON, G. and VERNON, D.F. (1977). *The Psychology and Education of Gifted Children.* London: Methuen.

WARNOCK REPORT. GREAT BRITAIN. DEPARTMENT OF EDUCATION AND SCIENCE. COMMITTEE OF ENQUIRY INTO THE EDUCATION OF HANDICAPPED CHILDREN AND YOUNG PEOPLE (1978). *Special Educational Needs.* London: HMSO.

WILKINSON, A. (1979). 'Assessing language development: The Crediton Project', *Language for Learning,* **1**, 2.

WILKINSON, A. and HANNA, P. (1979). 'Style in children's writing': The Crediton Project, *Language for Learning,* **1**, 2.

WILKINSON, A. and HANNA, P. (1980). 'The development of style in children's writing', *Educational Review,* **32**, 2.

WITTY, P. (Ed) (1951). *The Gifted Child.* Boston: Heath & Co.

WOOD, R. and NAPTHALI, N.A. (1975). 'Assessment in the classroom: what do teachers look for?', *Brit. J. Educ. Studies,* **1**, 3.

Index